"I Told My Mind To Shut The F*ck Up!"

...and then I saw what was possible.

Greg Winick

Copyright © 2012 Greg Winick
All rights reserved.

No part of this book may be reproduced, scanned or distributed in any printed or electronic form without permission. Please do not participate or encourage piracy of copyrighted materials in violation of the author's rights. Purchase only authorized editions.

Winick, Greg
"I Told My Mind To Shut The F*ck Up!"

ISBN: 147011741X
ISBN-13: 9781470117412

Createspace, Charleston, SC
Printed in the United States of America
First Edition

Table of Contents

Introduction i
The Making of a Problem 1
The Making of an Identity. 9
Our Dual Consciousness. 37
The Child Is the Father of the Man. 61
Awakening from the Mind-created Story 77
Living with Awareness 87
Find the Power to Create 115
The Mind-created Drama 129
Falling Back to Negative Stories. 159
How to Get What You Want 181
Jesse's Recovery 199
Scars 217

Introduction

I went to the bank the other day to withdraw money. I didn't have to actually walk into the branch because the cash machine is outside. I walked up to it, and the man in front of me was mad.

"This is bullshit," he said. He was a middle-aged white guy like me, so he must have assumed we were the same. He saw me behind him, and he shared his gripe.

"I have to choose English on this thing. This is America, isn't it?" He waited for me to respond. He needed me to agree that he was labeling a real problem, but I just gave him a half smile then took my turn on the machine. What an ass, I thought. He's getting cash from a machine, probably driving home in a new car to find his house with air conditioning and cable television waiting for him, yet he found a problem in his life. He has to click an extra button on the cash machine, and he is inconvenienced for one second. Poor guy.

It is difficult for me to hear people complaining about silly things. I realize he is unconscious, walking around listening to his mind as it finds things to call problems.

Likewise with Facebook. People are compelled to share the story of their life—it is like being addicted to heroin, but instead, Facebookers are looking for an approval fix. My friend Allison posts, "My wedding's next Friday, can't wait." A whole bunch of people like her status. They post back. "Congratulations Allison." "Enjoy every minute of it." "You deserve all the best." Because she is getting married she thinks she is supposed to be happy. And do you know why she is right? Because everyone agrees with her. Conversely, John is stuck in a traffic jam. He posts from his cell phone, "Backed up at the Lincoln Tunnel for over an hour now." His friends validate his belief that he is dealing with a problem. "That sucks, buddy." "I feel your pain." John has sufficient agreement that being stuck in the traffic jam is not a good thing, and of course it isn't.

Me, I have a problem that I consider to be much bigger than John's traffic situation. If I posted my problem, everyone would post back, "I'm so sorry." We are all praying for you." "We love you." And I would feel loved, and I would feel justified that what is happening in my life is really a problem—and that justification would only add to my suffering.

I have been living in the rehab hospital for over a month now. I am not the patient. I am a father who sleeps on a chair next to his son's bed every night. There are other fathers like me here. I befriended a man named Tony. I don't think that's his real name because he is Korean and doesn't speak English very well. I doubt Korean parents

Introduction

name their children Tony, but that's what everybody calls him here. Tony is here to speak to his seventeen-year-old son, Alex. Alex can't answer him back. Alex was in a jet-ski accident where he was hit in the head and spent ten minutes underwater before his friends noticed him. Alex can't move any part of his body. He cannot speak, and he is fed through a tube. All Alex can do is blink. Tony has spent weeks trying to interpret meaning from Alex's blinks but has been unsuccessful.

Tony is distraught, and he walks outside to the front of the hospital to smoke a cigarette every twenty minutes, and then he walks back in again, coughing his head off. I don't know how to help Tony. I want to. I feel fortunate to be able to converse with my son.

My son, Jesse, cannot walk or sit up. He is fed through a tube like Alex, and as hard as he tries to swallow on his own, he cannot do it. Not being able to swallow causes him to drool, and I spend a lot of my time suctioning saliva out of his mouth so he doesn't slobber all over himself. Jesse has a trach in his throat and a tube delivers oxygen to his lungs. His mind has not been affected by his ordeal, and he is aware of what has happened to him.

I am holding on to the possibility that Jesse will heal. My entire life seems to be hanging on that tiny thread of possibility. Our current situation can easily be labeled as a problem. My mind tells me it is. Talking about it with others and getting their agreement is only useful for proving that I am right about being upset.

• • •

I don't presume to be qualified to tell you how you should live your life. I have read many books' introductions, in which authors list their qualifications for writing about a certain subject. I have only one qualification. I have lived through my share of suffering. Not as much as some, but enough to know what suffering is. I have had the luxury of intense suffering to bring me into a state of conscious awareness.

This book is the story of my life. Therefore, I call it an autobiography. The lessons I offer along the way, however, may dispel some common misperceptions about life. I learned a lot from teachers of motivational psychology, consciousness philosophies, and New Age practices. Not only have I read all the books and taken all the courses, but I have led a life that has forced me more than once to walk the walk of the enlightened individual. Most of the concepts in this book are not mine—I am drawing on the teachings and my own interpretations of books I read and workshops and seminars I attended.

Nevertheless, I have added several distinctions to clarify these existing concepts. This is my modest attempt to share some of the ideas I credit for helping me survive the worst of my ordeals.

Chapter 1
The Making of a Problem

I am absorbed in the drama of the situation in which I find myself. My stomach is in knots, and I haven't been able to eat. I can't sleep without horrific thoughts entering my head. I can't think about anything else. I can't go to work. I can't deal with people. I can't remove myself from this state of panic.

Imagine you have been married for seventeen years and have a fifteen-year-old son. Imagine you are successful and happy with your life. Then imagine, three months ago, that some of the best doctors in the country told you your wife has to have a large kidney tumor removed. Moreover, it must be removed right away so she has time to recover before enduring a second surgery that will remove her entire pancreas, because there are many large tumors in that organ, as well.

And then imagine, while grappling with the proposition of your wife undergoing two major surgeries, that you encounter a problem that is even bigger.

• • •

At the same time your wife is panicking about her health, your teenage son is diagnosed with tumors in his brain and spine. Imagine that his doctors describe the brain tumor as a "big one," and his spinal tumor as the "biggest spinal tumor they had ever seen." Imagine the doctors telling you there is a high probability that your son will be totally paralyzed. Imagine receiving input from another specialist that your little boy, your baby, the love of your life, has tumors that are inoperable.

If you can imagine all this, which many people cannot unless tragic things have happened to them, then you can imagine what it is like to be me in September of 2010.

These problems are real because they are happening to my family, but I have another problem that is just as real. This other problem is with me—specifically, how I am dealing with the situation, and how I am reacting to my family's problems. I am not being the strong, confident man I need to be, I want to be. I am not being the man who handles these problems for my family. I am not being the man who figures a way out of this predicament, and even if it is beyond my power to solve, I am being a weak, fragile, nervous wreck who is not helping anybody.

My wife, Cathy, at least has a prognosis of survival. Jesse's brain and spinal tumors are an immediate priority. I left work two weeks ago to have Jesse checked out by the doctors at the National Cancer Institute. Those doctors gave me their opinions, and now I am standing in front of my house with the phone in my hand thinking about who to call next, and who will point me in the right direction. I need advice from someone more qualified than me. My friends don't know what to say to me. They want to help but are uncomfortable talking to me about it. I can feel that. I can also tell that anyone who hears about this situation is thankful it is not happening to them. They are at home, hugging their own children and thanking God they are not me. As for my family, they get upset when I call them because they love Jesse, too. They don't know what to do, either. My parents and my brother and sisters are feeling my pain, but not how I feel it.

This kind of pain is foreign to me. I believed that I suffered in the past. I thought I always had more difficulties in my life than most people. But this is different. This pain won't let go of me, not for a minute. I lie awake at night trying to watch the TV, but I can only watch certain shows. *Seinfeld* is light and doesn't draw me into my troubles. But if I try to watch the news, I see the Dow Jones plummeting, and I think, "Who gives a shit?" I listen to commentators talk about how to fix the country, and I can't believe people expend so much passion and energy defending their points. Don't they know how silly they are? Don't they know they should be happy for their health and should celebrate every moment their family is not being attacked by tumors?

In the middle of the night, I stare at the dark wall next to my bed and try to focus on it. I can't stop the thoughts from coming in. The thoughts are screaming at me: Your son is going to be paralyzed! You have to tell him that! I scream back at my thoughts: No! I will find someone that can fix him. You don't know who you're dealing with! Fuck you, thoughts! Shut the fuck up!

People are telling me everything will be OK. What the hell do they know? They weren't there when I spoke to the doctors—if they were, they would be just as horrified as I am. People are telling me they are praying for me. I'm praying too: Please, please God, help Jesse. I know I'm a Jew who hasn't gone to temple in over thirty years, but my wife goes to church every Sunday, and my son goes to a Catholic high school. That's got to count for something. I've never hurt a soul in my entire life. I try to help everyone I know. You know I'm a good man. Please help me, God. Haven't I suffered enough in this life? I've walked through twenty years of surgeries with Cathy. I've had a tougher childhood than most people I know. I've had to pick myself up and reinvent myself over and over again in this life. Am I supposed to undergo the most unbearable suffering imaginable?

Is that who I'm supposed to be, the man who can endure anything?

• • •

Cathy and I are both teachers. The school year just started. I have to go in to work, plan lessons, grade papers, and act enthusiastic about teaching.

I can't even fathom it. I am afraid I will lose my job if I don't go back soon. How long can I stay out of work without losing my job? I need the medi-

The Making of a Problem

cal benefits. How can I go in, though? How can I face anyone without crying? A few months ago, I was telling my work friends about how Cathy might have to have her pancreas removed. They all said how sorry they were. Now I am telling them about my son's crisis. It doesn't sound believable. Who has these kinds of medical problems? I feel like I am double-dipped in shit.

I'm like a scared kid. I need an adult to talk to, but there are no adults. People have always shared their opinions about what I should or shouldn't do, but not this time. I can't remember a time when there wasn't at least one person willing to give advice to me. No one I know would dare make a declaration about what the right thing to do is here. The choice of who operates on Jesse is Cathy's and mine, and we have not yet met a doctor who feels confident about handling the surgery.

There must be some genius doctor in this world who can make me feel confident that I am giving Jesse his best shot at a positive outcome. We have spent twenty years reading doctors' poker faces, and so far, our decisions about who to use have been perfect, and I mean *perfect*. I can tell when doctors know what to do, and also when they don't have a clue. Because of a rare, hereditary condition, Cathy has had dozens of serious surgeries, and every single one of them has worked out flawlessly. She has retained almost-perfect health over all these years, but even Cathy has never had a prognosis like Jesse's. I can't help thinking that Cathy and I have been walking in between the raindrops for too long, and we are about to get really wet.

I must act. I know that. I must free myself from this state of panic so I can think. I must do whatever is possible to save my son and my wife. They must be in the best possible hands for dealing with their serious health issues. I need my actions to be the right ones, because there is no room for mistakes, and the wrong decisions will have lifelong consequences. I know all of this.

All of these problems are huge. They are the biggest problems I have ever encountered in my life. I don't know if they are even solvable. To me, my problems are bigger than any other problems in the entire world. All of a sudden, every other thing that I thought I cared about is gone. I will do anything. I will leave my job. I will sell my house. I will use every penny I have to fix this thing. I will fly around the world, seeking out the best doctors. I will do whatever is necessary, but first I have to get out of my head.

The words people are telling me, "Everything will be OK," are not helping me. The prayers people are giving me are not helping, either. I need more than pity and prayers. I need empowerment.

• • •

Using what the doctors told me, I have formed a story in my head. The story in my head does not allow me to believe in a positive outcome. I consider my circumstances to be a problem.

The Making of a Problem

My biggest problem, however, is that I am considering my family's health issues to actually be "problems" rather than obstacles to overcome. My perspective on the situation is actually the only problem over which I have control. I am trapped in a mind-created story. I am trapped in my mind's dramatic interpretation of my current situation. As I grapple with my dilemma, I realize that I have always been predisposed to consider the circumstances of my life to be a problem, and seeing life this way has never allowed me to get what I want.

So, I have learned to fight my natural inclinations in order to create new possibilities for myself, and I desperately need to do that now.

Chapter 2
The Making of an Identity

Your First Identity Is Given

I was born in New Jersey. My parents told me I was an American because that's where New Jersey is located. My parents also told me that I was Jewish because they were Jewish. My father told me he won second place in the Mr. Universe contest in 1963, so I was the son of second-place Mr. Universe. Whenever I told someone that my father was second-place Mr. Universe, they would always ask, "What happened to you?" I once asked a kid why he said that, and he told me, "Because you're so skinny and small."

So I was a skinny, small, Jewish, American kid from New Jersey whose father was Mr. Universe. (I usually left out the second place part.) Those were the first stories I created about myself when I was a little kid. If someone were to ask me who I was, that is what I would have said. I created those stories about myself because that is what people told me, and I believed them.

• • •

I grew up in a town called Nutley, New Jersey, whose population at the time was 99 percent Italian. They were not Jewish like me. They were all

Christians, and I felt different from most kids in my school. There were two Jews in my school: me and my little brother. I would tell people how my father was Mr. Universe because I thought that made me interesting. Those were my credentials at the time, making me worth talking to. I wanted to share my little story with the world so that people would like me. Also, it was pretty easy to wind up in a fight in my school, so I figured that maybe nobody would mess with a skinny little Jewish kid if they knew his father was Mr. Universe.

Your Second Identity Is Chosen

My *identity*, or the story of who I am, was further established as I interacted with more people in the world. My home life was difficult. My parents always fought and were headed for divorce. By sixth grade, I was not what most people would consider a model student. I came to school without a lunch and without milk money. I never did my homework. I never studied or brought home any books. I didn't pay attention in class, and I didn't really care about school at all.

My sixth grade teacher was Mrs. Kostyra. She was in her sixties and probably planning her retirement. She was strict, and students considered her the toughest out of the three sixth grade teachers in our elementary school. Mrs. Kostyra would get mad at me. She would send notes home about me not having any lunch money. She would ask me why my clothes were all wrinkled and tell me that I needed

The Making of an Identity

to wash every day before coming to school—she told me things nobody really told me at home. And she noticed that I didn't really care about school.

At the time, I just thought she was a pain in the ass. I considered her the old, grumpy, strict teacher that nobody liked, but I had to deal with her until the sixth grade was over. My parents thought of her in the same way, and they would get mad when she sent notes home.

My elementary school kept us until the sixth grade. Like many other school districts, we would go to a middle school for seventh and eighth grade and then to high school. As I said before, I was not a good student, but I did articulate my thoughts in class. I took part in the discussions, and I learned how to read, write, and do math like everybody else. I was lazy and lacked direction, but I wasn't stupid. Mrs. Kostyra must have realized this because she did something I didn't expect. When it came time for her to recommend students for placement into the seventh grade honors program, she put me on her list.

I was placed in all honors courses. I didn't realize this until I found myself in classes with all the smartest kids in the school. There I was, a kid who never studied, never did homework, and barely even picked up a book, trying to keep up with all the honor students. I struggled. I got low grades, and cursed Mrs. Kostyra's judgment. I knew she didn't like me, and wondered if she was trying to torture me.

I was able to keep up and squeaked by with mostly C's in my classes. When I arrived at high school, I wound up dropping all my advanced courses and putting myself in what they called the "dummy" classes. There I was able to do well without ever studying or ever picking up a book. I graduated high school without putting forth any academic effort whatsoever.

• • •

Many years later, I realized that this experience led me to a conclusion about myself. Even though I was not a good student and thought school was unimportant, I knew that I was smart. I knew it absolutely, based on one thing: Mrs. Kostyra placed me into the advanced classes. She wouldn't have done that if she didn't think I was smart.

To tell you the truth, I don't really know why she did it. Maybe it was a mistake, but subconsciously, I interpreted it as her recognition of my intelligence. In other words, I created a story that Mrs. Kostyra put me in the advanced classes because I was smart, and based on it, I made a decision about myself and my capabilities in the seventh grade.

What Is a Story?

The dictionary definition of a story is an account or recital of an event or a series of events, either true or fictitious. So, in our lives, stories are important:

The Making of an Identity

Something happens→
We interpret meaning→
We make a decision about ourselves.

The events in our lives are real. We decide what our life means, and who we are. For example, someone might say to you, "You are boring." That's real, but where you take it from there is up to you. You might interpret it to mean that the speaker thinks you are being boring right now, or it might mean that they always think you're boring, or it might mean that everyone thinks you're boring, or it might mean that you are actually boring. Whatever you decide it means will depend on you, but whatever you decide, it's only an interpretation. If your house burns down, you could interpret the event as unlucky, or you might decide you are lucky because you were not in it.

Your interpretations of the things that happen in your life are flexible. The only thing that is real in your life is what actually happens; everything else in your life is a mind-created story.

People make all kinds of decisions about themselves based on their interpretation of what happens to them. They decide if they are good-looking or ugly. These decisions are subjective, but most of the time they are confirmed by others' agreement. If you ever had a friend come to you and say, "I'm ugly," your first reaction will probably be to say, "That's not true," because actually it isn't; it's a made-up decision based on something that happened, how someone reacted or what someone said.

These decisions are the very things that govern how far we get in life, how happy we are, and how successful we become. These decisions we make about ourselves are all stories. We live in our story as if it were true.

It's like what happened to me. I interpreted Mrs. Kostyra's actions to mean she thought I was smart. I don't really know what she was thinking, but subconsciously, I chose my story—and my story said I was smart.

Perhaps Mrs. Kostyra was a person who knew how to inspire children. Perhaps she intentionally tried to influence my life. She was obviously able to have a positive influence on her own daughter's life. Her daughter created a billion-dollar business. Mrs. Kostyra, my sixth grade teacher at Lincoln Elementary School, in Nutley, New Jersey, had a daughter who would later become quite famous—her daughter's name is Martha Stewart.

The Making of an Identity

My father, Jerry Winick, won several bodybuilding titles in the 1960s. He was most famous for placing second in the 1963 IFBB Mr. Universe contest.

Mrs. Kostyra, my sixth grade teacher, and her daughter Martha Stewart.

Your Story Shapes Your Behavior

The events that took place during my adolescent years caused me to create a deep-rooted, dramatic story about myself that would shape all my future actions.

There were many differences between my parents and the parents of other kids I knew. My parents seemed younger and hipper than others. My parents were Democrats while it seemed like everyone else's were Republicans. My parents were into self-enlightenment and EST training (a popular seminar program at the time.) They would smoke pot in the house with their friends. Not that they were hippies or flower children, but at the time, they were discovering who they were themselves. They were like teenagers with kids. My parents had conflicting ideas about how I was to be raised. My father thought it was funny to have a seven-year-old kid who would say "fuck" or "shit" in the course of a normal conversation with people. My mother didn't think it was so funny, and this was one of a million other things that would cause Jerry and Sheila to fight.

When I was young, my father, Jerry, had a job as a union dress presser. He worked in a dress factory for fourteen years, and he was paid by the piece—that is to say, he was paid per dress, not hourly. Being paid like that allowed him the freedom to finish his work for the day at his own pace and then depart when he was done. He said it was like being paid for doing his own portion of the business, and this policy made his profession more lucrative. After they started paying the dress pressers by the hour, Jerry lost his freedom at work and wound up quitting. My father had no tolerance for being taken advantage

The Making of an Identity

of by a boss. That was the only full-time job I ever remember him having for any substantial period of time. After he left that job, he would stay out late playing poker with his friends, and my mother didn't like it one bit.

I thought my father was cool. Maybe it was because he let me do whatever I wanted. My mother would nag me to do things like clean my room or do my homework, but since my father didn't really care, I would get away with murder. I would often hear my mother complaining to my aunts about my father, which would make me mad. I made up a story that Sheila didn't really understand Jerry.

My mother found it difficult to enforce any rules with me. Instead, she started drifting away from my father, and I made up a story that she drifted away from me, too.

• • •

I have a brother, Keith, who is two years younger than me, and a sister, Kim, who is five years younger. I also have another sister, Michelle, who was born after my father remarried, but she was not part of my youth. My relationship with my siblings has always been very strong. I think we built up a cohesive bond growing up the way we did, listening to our parents battle all the time, and as a result, we share similar insecurities.

One of the distinct memories my brother and I share about being young and living with our parents was never having any food in the house. We saw that our relatives had dinner every night. My parents rarely went food shopping and rarely prepared meals for us. My brother and I remember scavenging through the house looking for anything to eat, and often we would go across town to our aunt's house and eat as much as we could. Usually we would have bowl after bowl of cereal until we were full. I remember one of my uncles getting annoyed by our eating behavior. I created a story that it wasn't fair, always having to nose around in other people's refrigerators to eat. I always thought it was unfair that I was forced to be a freeloader, and also that I was, indeed, a freeloader.

• • •

My mother had three sisters who lived in neighboring towns. They were all married with children, and I had nine cousins who were around my age. My mother's side of the family was very close, and we were together for every birthday party, Chanukah, Passover, and New Year's Eve, and at least one dinner a week. I considered my relatives different from our immediate family. All three of my uncles were successful, and so my cousins and their families were a stabilizing force in my life. All our clothes were hand-me-downs from our cousins. When my father was out of work, my aunts and uncles would offer to help us. Even though my own family always had money issues, I felt like I was still a solid member of a well-to-do family. I knew that somehow I would be taken care of if my parents were unable to do it. Despite this feeling, I still created a story that I had it harder than most people.

The Making of an Identity

Not only did I feel different than the other kids at school, I felt different from my cousins, too. My brother and I were close with them, and we benefited from their financial security. We instinctually developed expectations about ourselves based on our cousins' expectations for their own lives. They all planned to go to college, be rich, get married, and have nice houses, and so did we. We were like them because we were related to them. The story I created was that I was supposed to be like them.

• • •

When I was thirteen, my parents finally got divorced. My father told my mother that he cheated on her. I knew my father. He thought he was an enlightened person after taking the EST training, so he thought he could say or do anything as long as he was truthful about it. Although he knew he fucked up, and felt horrible about it, he thought he would be rewarded for his honesty.

For my mother, this was the last straw. My father didn't work, he stayed out late playing poker every night with his buddies, cheated on her, and was argumentative. That was her story about what happened.

My father was broken up over losing his wife. He even seemed suicidal. He had a different story in which he wasn't such a bad husband, but I accepted my mother's version anyway, and it became the "real" one. She had given her family her story of why she was leaving him, and of course they all believed it. My mother wanted nothing to do with him, and since we were all so close with her side of the family, my father really had no one on his side.

Even though I knew that my mother was probably right to leave him, I couldn't just abandon him in the state he was in. Somebody had to take care of him. I made up a story that I was someone who saw when people were in need.

• • •

After the divorce, my mother moved in with one of her sisters. She took my eight-year-old sister with her, and my father took my brother and me into his apartment. The relationship between my mother and me was not good to begin with, and she knew I would be impossible to separate from my father. This choice to live with him was mine, and my mother knew she couldn't stop me.

I knew he had made mistakes, but I still idolized him. My brother, who was eleven, probably had the more difficult choice. He chose to stay with the men, my father and me, because it seemed logical.

After my parents sold their house, my father's portion of the proceeds seemed like a lot of money at the time, but he had already taken out loans against the anticipated sale. He didn't have a job, but he thought he could make a living playing poker in local games.

Jerry claimed to be a pretty good card player. He would show me records that he kept of the game statistics, which showed a profit every time. I found out many years later that he showed those to my

The Making of an Identity

mother, too, and they were complete bullshit. It took him just a few months to lose all the money we had. He blamed his inability to win on my mother. He was lost without her. He said he just didn't have his head screwed on right anymore.

Being a single parent was too much for Jerry, and our apartment was a pigsty. One day we had a sink full of dishes, and instead of washing them, Jerry told us to just throw them all in the garbage. We did. He said he would just buy new ones. But he didn't. He left the apartment every day, saying, "I'm going out to find a bag of money."

I guess the idea of getting a job and working every day never occurred to him. He went out to bars every night and left us alone in the apartment. He needed adults to talk to, and he didn't really have any good friends. He only knew guys from poker games and the candy store where he hung out at all day. He dated several women at a time, and came in late at night with one of them. I would hear them in the living room, and not be able to sleep. This made me uncomfortable, but the next morning, my father would tell me about it like I was his friend, not his son.

I didn't want to hear it. I created a story that my father thought my brother and I were his roommates instead of his sons.

• • •

I met two friends who lived in our apartment complex. Rick and Dave were two years older than I, seniors at my high school. They smoked a lot of pot, and I would smoke it with them. I knew Jerry didn't care because he smoked pot all the time. In fact, I can't ever remember a time when he forbade us from smoking pot, even as small children. Keith and I started hanging out with the older boys, and soon we were drinking beer and smoking pot all the time.

At the bus stop every day before school, I smoked a joint. I started getting a reputation as a burnout, which was not the worst thing you could be back then. In 1979 there were plenty of burnouts. I pretty much kept quiet in class and was stoned most of the time. I breezed through my classes without ever bringing home a book, studying, or doing any homework. I knew kids in high school whose parents would look at their report cards, and punish them for getting poor grades. I made up a story that my parents didn't give a shit.

• • •

After never locating that bag of money Jerry went out to find every day, he finally signed us up for food stamps and welfare. The first of the month, Keith and I would push a shopping cart down the railroad tracks behind our apartments to get to the supermarket. When a fourteen-year-old and a twelve-year-old do the food shopping, one can imagine what we would buy. We got plenty of cake, chips, ice cream, TV dinners, and canned goods. We were used to eating cereal for breakfast, so we would get plenty of that. We never bought meat or anything that required cooking. We thought we were lucky to be able to eat whatever we wanted.

The Making of an Identity

I didn't learn until much later in life that most people ate very differently from us. A family having dinner together was a television fiction—Keith and I didn't know people actually ate together in real life. I also never learned any table manners. I had no idea how to hold a knife and fork. I had to learn a lot of things as an adult, and much later I created a story that it was not fair that I received no guidance in simple etiquette.

• • •

Keith and I got into all kinds of trouble. We would go into the rough sections of Newark to buy drugs with our new friends that drove cars. One time a pot dealer took our money and told us to get lost. When we disputed the deal, he threw a wine bottle that smashed all over the inside of my friend's car. It was pretty scary. Another time, one guy punched my friend, who was driving, and a bunch of other guys started trying to jump into the car. My friend peeled out to get away and drove over someone's foot as we sped off.

We put ourselves in all sorts of dangerous situations. We would get stoned and jump on and off the moving train cars. We vandalized apartments. We broke into unrented apartments in the complex and partied in them. We stole food from convenience stores and supermarkets. One time Keith got arrested for shoplifting at the Pathmark. No one was home when they called our apartment, so one of my uncles had to come and pick him up. Keith was a cute, scared, little kid so the Pathmark didn't press charges. I made up a story that we were juvenile delinquents.

• • •

One time we were running around the apartments and causing a ruckus. A couple of older guys ran out of their apartment after us. They chased my brother and me and two of our friends across the courtyard and into our building. I fumbled to get my keys out in what seemed like forever, opened the door, and we all hid in the closets and under the bed in our apartment. The three guys busted in, yelling, "Where are you? Whose apartment is this?" I came out from under the bed and yelled back at them. "This is our apartment, so get the fuck out!" Those three older men beat the living shit out of me in my own apartment. I remember trying to get myself into a ball so they wouldn't hit anything important, but they pounded me to a bloody pulp. My friends and my brother all stayed in their hiding places as it was happening, and when the men were done pummeling me, they ran out. I think they eventually realized they were beating up a little kid in his own home.

I told my father what had happened, and he seemed pissed at me for getting into this kind of trouble. I wanted him to go find those guys and kill them, but he didn't. I created a story that the world was dangerous, and nobody was going to look out for me, so I had to be careful.

• • •

The Making of an Identity

I know it seems like my father was a real shit back then, but that is not how I saw him. I was not mad at my father but furious with my mother. I blamed Sheila for everything, just as Jerry did. After my parents' divorce, I always blamed her. She wanted to end the marriage and he didn't. I was mad at her for breaking up our family. I was mad at her for not considering us kids. I felt like my life was not supposed to unfold like this. I was supposed to have a carefree existence like my cousins had. Most of all I was mad at how my mother reacted toward me. I felt like she couldn't get over the fact that I chose to live with my father. She was mad at me because I was on his side. That's how it was—us against her.

I had chosen to be with my father because he showed more affection to me than my mother did. He told me how proud he was of me, and even though he was often absent, he never stopped telling me how great I was. He wore his emotions on his sleeve, and when he was fucking up, he knew it, and he would cry about it. I spent many years believing that my mother really didn't love me at all. She seemed cold toward me. It was as if I reminded her so much of my father that she hated me like she hated him.

My father fueled my story about my mother. When they sold the house, my father got thirty percent of the proceeds and my mother got seventy percent. He would tell me how unfair that was because he now had two kids to support while my mother only had my sister. Jerry always found reasons to be the victim. I believed his stories. He let me develop a hatred for my mother. My hating her fueled and justified his own story that Sheila victimized us all, and the story I created about my mother ran strong and deep.

• • •

Money was a huge issue because the rent was always late and we never knew where we would get money for food. My father usually kept our welfare checks. He would give us a little money to buy lunch at school, and my brother and I figured out which stores would take food stamps so we could buy snacks. My father would gamble away the rest of our cash in the poker games. Our bills were consistently late, and the phone and electricity were shut off until we made the payments. I created a story that we were poor.

• • •

I took a job selling newspaper subscriptions door to door. I worked for a man named Jimmy Botbyle. Jimmy would pick up a crew of kids after school, drop us off for three or four hours at a time in different towns, and we would canvass the area. We knocked on doors and talked people into subscribing to the *Herald News* for eight weeks for only one dollar per week. It was a good deal and easy to sell.

I figured out quickly what to say and do in order to convince people to buy my product. I was lucky enough to have immediate success, and in the first few weeks of selling papers, I was already getting

The Making of an Identity

more orders than most of the other kids. I was lucky, because by having immediate success, my mind was able to create a story that it could easily be done. If I saw that I could do something, I knew that I could repeat my actions and keep doing it.

I knocked on every door in northern New Jersey, literally. If you lived in Passaic, Essex, or Bergen County in New Jersey during the late seventies and early eighties, I knocked on your door at least once. I wound up being the best newspaper subscription salesmen the *Herald News* ever had. I knew I could keep knocking on doors until I got what I wanted, and unlike the other kids, I would run from door to door to hit as many as I could. I got ten times as many sales as the other kids every single day. The other kids got paychecks of about thirty or forty dollars per week. My checks were consistently over three hundred.

I worked six days a week, every day after school and on Saturday mornings. My boss said I was a real phenomenon, and I felt great about it. My brother and my father felt great about it too, because we really did need the money. I remember feeling like a big shot because I was actually making more money than my mother, who was working as a dental assistant. I created a story about myself that I was a great salesman.

• • •

I never went to family gatherings anymore. The single time I saw them after the divorce, my relatives had plenty to say about what a loser my father was. I didn't want to hear it, and didn't go to any more family events after that. My brother continued, though, and visited my mother every week. One time, my father and I picked him up from a Chanukah party; we were waiting outside in the car, and one of my cousins came out with all the gifts my aunts had purchased for me. They wanted me to come inside, but I wouldn't. I had chosen a side and I was sticking to it. It felt weird, but I wanted my father to know that he wasn't alone. I created a story that I was a loyal son.

• • •

Eventually my father started dating someone more seriously, and he slept at her house almost every night. He decided my brother and I could take care of ourselves, so we did. I was still making money selling newspaper subscriptions after school. In fact, I was getting record-breaking numbers week after week. I was able to do so well that, after banking most of my checks for a six-month period, I saved over five thousand dollars. I felt sure I would grow up to be a millionaire.

Despite my difficult situation, I was determined to make a success of myself. My father, however, who never kept up with the bills, approached me one day with some bad news. He told me that we would be evicted from the apartment the next day if we didn't pay at least three months back rent and a bunch of other bills. He took my entire five thousand dollars. Coincidentally, when we went to the bank to withdraw the money, my mother was there

The Making of an Identity

in the parking lot. She saw me crying in the car and came over to me. I didn't want to tell her what was happening. I didn't want to give her and her family any more fuel against us.

As a result of this experience, I created a story that any money I made would all be taken away from me.

• • •

A few months later we got evicted from our apartment anyway. My father took some work driving a limousine. Getting evicted from our apartment after two years really seemed like a defeat in our fight against Sheila. We scrounged up enough money for rent and a security deposit on another apartment on the other side of town.

My brother and I insisted that we stay in the same town so we wouldn't have to switch high schools. The new apartment was right down the street from my mother and my sister and right up the street from my aunt's house. I remember feeling more secure knowing that my relatives lived so close. I started hanging out with my cousins again, and I would even run into my mother once in a while. My relationship with my mother's side of the family began to repair itself.

The new apartment really turned into mine and my brother's own apartment. My father didn't even have a bed there. I had one bedroom and Keith had the other. I was still working every day, and I was making good money. Our rent was only three hundred a month, and I was making three hundred a week, so I got my own checking account and started paying the rent, the utilities, and all the other bills myself. It really wasn't too hard. I still had money left over for food and lunch money for both Keith and myself. We were behind on the bills sometimes, but we were keeping up a lot better than we were before. Sometimes my father would give us some money, but for the most part we were on our own. I developed a strong story that I really didn't need to depend on anyone.

• • •

My brother and I stayed in that apartment until my senior year of high school. Our place became a real bachelor pad, and we had many parties with our cousins and our friends. I worked six days a week all throughout high school, and I developed a story that I was a responsible person. I never played any sports or did a lot of the things common among high school kids, but I did have a lot of fun.

I had a good friend who worked with me on the sales crew after school. Eric would work one side of the street and I would work the other. Our objective was to get sales, but our main objective was to meet girls. We would do our cute little presentation at people's doorsteps, hoping that one of us would run across a house with some teenage girls in it. Getting their phone numbers became just as important as sales, and we met a lot of girls that way.

Eric lived with his mother and his little sister. We were the same age, but he didn't go to school at all. He had dropped out of seventh grade, and

The Making of an Identity

his mother had moved through different parts of the country, following different boyfriends. Eric's mother didn't have a man at the time, so she collected welfare checks and whatever Eric earned. Eric worked in a fast food restaurant all day, and he sold newspaper subscriptions with me in the evenings. Eric gave his mother both of his paychecks every week to pay the bills. I used my money to pay the bills, too, but Eric and I had many differences in the expectations we had for our lives based on the stories we had created about ourselves. I felt a kinship with Eric because of our similar circumstances, but I knew something about my circumstance was better. I was going to graduate high school and go to college. Eric had always been poor, and he had no other family at all. I had an extended family that I could always fall back on, and I still considered myself a middle class kid who would eventually see better times. The image or story that I had about myself would eventually make all the difference in my life.

• • •

My brother and I were completely unsupervised for most of my high school years, but when I graduated high school, Keith moved into my mother's apartment for his junior and senior year. After graduation, I never lived with my mother or my father again.

I want to be perfectly clear about something. I was not an abused child. I remember two aspects about being young. I ultimately knew that both of my parents loved me. Underneath my anger for my mother, I knew she never did anything to intentionally hurt me. My parents lived through a nasty divorce that caused them both a lot of suffering, and the suffering we went through was an unintentional consequence. When I was a teenager, my parents were so lost in their own stories that they were barely capable of taking care of themselves, let alone us, but I wouldn't be able to understand that until many years later.

My parents each remarried, and I felt like such a hindrance to their new spouses. Gabe married my mother, and Karen married my father, but really, what was their obligation to us? Both of my parents needed a spouse because they struggled to support themselves alone, and I was happy they found people they loved, but I did hold on to a story that my brother and I were baggage. My parents' lives completely stabilized after they both got married. My mother's husband Gabe owned a successful insurance agency, and he was also the owner and manager of a large apartment complex. My father's wife Karen proved to be a positive influence, and my father worked steadily throughout their marriage and eventually found his calling as a professional artist. My father was never again the man he had been when I was a teenager.

• • •

Now, my story was not just that I was a skinny, Jewish boy from New Jersey whose father was Mr. Universe. Of course that story will always stay with me, but the story of my identity became much more

The Making of an Identity

complex. Like a lot of people, I developed a fictional drama that I called my life story. From that time, I created what I call negative and positive stories about myself. I was now a person who survived a rough childhood. Based on what happened to me when I was a teenager, I made all kinds of new decisions about myself. I decided I had shitty parents. I decided I had it harder than everybody else. I decided that I had a bad start in life. I was also the guy who could support himself and his brother through most of high school, and I was a great salesman who could sell to anyone. I decided I could talk people into doing what I wanted, and I did. I made those decisions about myself subconsciously, based on what happened at that time.

All these decisions would shape and restrict my future actions. I would act as a person who had those things happen to him. Perhaps if I had grown up under different circumstances, I would have become a completely different person, for better or worse. I let my story completely define me. I allowed my mind to control how I felt about my life. Mostly what I interpreted from my childhood experience was that I was supposed to be mad about it. My mind would always gravitate toward the negative story—things that happened to me meant I should be angry—and so underneath, I was always angry. I was always compelled to tell my story, mostly as a way to get girls to like me. The girls would sympathize with me. I figured out early that being a person who has overcome great obstacles was a great way of impressing people, so I used my story as a way of getting what I wanted. Girls would give me the agreement I needed to confirm that my sob story was true. It was like going on Facebook and writing, "Look at what happened to me," and having people respond, "Yes, you had it hard," thus confirming my belief that I should be angry.

I was right in feeling that way. I was right because others told me I was right. That made it true.

• • •

My parents have their own stories about what happened during those years, and I could not see how they were not the same as mine. My mind created many stories about who I was, and I could have lived in a story that I was loved, and that my situation during my teenage years was unfortunate but not intentional—that story was just as apparent as the story that I was neglected and living in poverty for a long time. Both stories existed for me simultaneously, and I see now how I had the opportunity to choose which story I would embellish. My mind focused more on the negative aspects of my youth rather than the positive ones, because that is what the mind does. It finds problems.

I thought I had suffered as a young person. My mind told me that my problems back then were the biggest problems in the world. I know now that I had no idea what real suffering was. When I look back on those times now, I realize that my youth was really a magnificent experience.

The Making of an Identity

> *Negative stories* are beliefs about what is wrong in your life. You use them to tell yourself why you can't do something. Negative stories place limitations or restrictions on your life.
>
> *Positive stories* are beliefs about what is good in your life. They are stories about what you do well and why you are fortunate. Positive stories allow you to believe that you can do certain things.

Chapter 3
Our Dual Consciousness

Stories are created in the mind. You might say that the story lives in your mind, and it doesn't ever go away. It is there as a mechanism to protect you.

When I speak about the mind, some people are compelled to recall medical studies about how certain parts of the brain work or cite psychological studies on how the human mind actually works. Compelling arguments can be made about how those who claim to be enlightened thinkers are not actually correct. I would like to dispel that idea right now by proclaiming that everything I write about the mind and its workings can only be substantiated through intense observation. I am not saying that these ideas are true but rather they are just a way of looking at how you think and perceive things. My ideas are not *the* way to look at your life, rather they are *another* way to see things.

Thought and Awareness

First, we have to acknowledge that our thoughts are separate from who we are. In other words, there was me and there was my mind.

This is not an easy concept to grasp. If you really think about, there is a duality to your consciousness. You can be aware of a thought that comes into your head as if there was something within you that created the thought and something else in you that is aware of the thought. I was not my thoughts, or as Eckhart Tolle says, "You are not your mind." My mind—my thoughts—were reflex responses based on past experiences.

That's not how I saw it, though. If my mind told me I was supposed to do something, I believed it. Of course, we all have ignored our minds on occasion; anyone who has felt like yelling really loud in a library and didn't do it will agree. But the mind can be tricky. It can make up things about yourself and tell you to believe them. It wants to protect you. It doesn't want you to get hurt physically or emotionally. That's why the guy that got turned down the first time he asked a girl out on a date will forever be apprehensive. Every time he thinks about asking a girl out, he will have to either cave in to his fear of rejection, or ignore those thoughts and ask the girl out anyway.

The mind will always try to look out for you. It will tell you not to stand up and speak in front of a large group of people because you might say the wrong thing and get embarrassed. The mind is afraid of getting hurt—its job is to protect you—therefore the mind is more cautious than courageous, more pessimistic than optimistic. If you really look into your own mind, you will see that it tends to focus on more negative thoughts than positive ones.

Our Dual Consciousness

The mind is also repetitive. It will supply you with more thoughts about a subject or event than necessary. The mind never stops evaluating, judging, trying to solve the problems in your life, and creating stories about every single thing that happens to you. It is a big noise machine in your head that never shuts off. This is provable, because no matter how hard you try, you can almost never stop thinking. You can observe that most of the thoughts in your mind are repetitive and unnecessary.

• • •

This is a difficult concept to distill, so please forgive my redundancy, but often in telling my tale, I will refer to my mind as one part of me and my "self" or "I" as another. I know this may sound like I am describing a schizophrenic. To a certain degree, I am. Many mental illnesses can really be considered just more pronounced versions of what is normal among human beings.

This duality I am describing exists in everyone. To be absolutely clear, though, when I refer to my mind, I am referring to the mechanism within me that brings forth thoughts, memories, and emotions from my past. My mind also does the job of automatically interpreting everything that happens. These interpretations are what I am calling stories.

The "I," or self, is the part of me that has the ability to be aware of my thoughts and interpretations. The "I" has the ability to choose my actions. It's almost like a part of me is a machine and part of me isn't.

Stories Create Actions

The actions I took as a young adult were always driven by the stories I had created about myself in my youth.

I graduated high school, and since technically I was still in the custody of my father who earned barely any income, I was able to get financial aid that paid for everything. Dorm room, meals, tuition, books… The college was even required to give me a job on campus. It actually was a pretty great deal for me, and I could have listened to the positive story in my mind that said so, but my mind focused on the negative story instead. I decided that I was different from all the other college kids. I decided that I had it harder than all of them. They had a place to go home to on the weekends and holidays. They had parents who would give them money when they needed it and they had mothers that would do their laundry.

I decided that since I had struggled so hard to support myself in high school, I should party as much as possible. So I did. I joined a fraternity and made lots of friends, and I don't regret those days at all. But I was still mad about a lot of things—at least my mind always found problems, and told me that I should be mad. I still had to support myself. I didn't have a home to go back to during the breaks or in the summer. I stayed at my friends' houses, and when the dorms were closed, I lived out of my car. And that was kind of great at the time, too. I was young and free and I had a world of possibility in front of me.

Our Dual Consciousness

During that first college summer, I rented a house at the Jersey Shore. One of my fraternity brothers, Dave, had an idea that he and I would buy a hot dog pushcart. We thought we might be able to support ourselves with it.

We created a hot dog company, and here I learned that I could take an idea from my head and turn it into reality. I could create a possibility and live into it. Our plan was to put our hot dog cart on the boardwalk by the beach, so we did that, and it made money because we were the only food for sale on that section of the beach. We had a good location, and we made enough money in the first few weeks to buy another hot dog cart.

Then we wondered, "What if we put a cart outside of one of these popular Jersey Shore nightclubs?" We created the possibility that we could, so we approached the owner of a nightclub one night and they let us put a cart outside of their bar. We did that again with another bar, and again with another bar, and then we put two more carts on the boardwalk with our original one, and by the end of our first summer we owned and operated six hot dog pushcarts. The carts outside the bars did phenomenal. Our customers were drunk, and they would woof down as many hot dogs as they could to fill their stomachs and drink more. When the bars would close we would have huge lines of people wanting to eat before driving home. It took two people to run the cart when the line got that long. One of us would take the money and keep putting new hot dogs into the boiling dirty water. The other one would put hot dogs into buns and cover them with mustard, sauerkraut or onions. I got really good at it and learned how to line up as many as six buns up my arm and flip the hot dogs in, one at a time. Sometimes we would sell hot dogs so fast that people would bite into the ice cold ones that had just gone into the water. The people didn't care, though, because they were drunk. Almost overnight we became the biggest hot dog company at the Jersey Shore.

It was a great time. The shore house we rented became a hot dog warehouse. We had giant cans of mustard and sauerkraut and onions piled everywhere. Pallets of buns were delivered every morning, and we bought out the supermarket's entire aisle of chips and soda. We had three carts running all day at the beach and three carts running all night at the bars. My partner and I ran around stocking the carts, which were run by our frat brothers. We also went into the bars and drank every night. Everyone in town knew us. We were the hot dog guys, celebrities. Everywhere we would go, people would yell out, "Hey, it's the hot dog guys!" We met new girls every night. We ate hot dogs for breakfast, hung out at the beach all day and the bars all night, and made a fortune while we did it.

Having the hot dog company taught me some valuable lessons. I learned an important thing about how to accumulate money. It's really very simple: Earn more than you spend. But I didn't do that. We were selling five thousand hot dogs a week, along with chips and soda, and the profit margins were huge—but we went out to dinner every night and paid for all our friends. We bought drinks for everyone at the bars, and we lived it up. We spent every dime. The next summer we did the same thing, and after that summer, I didn't go back to college.

My mind told me I didn't need to go to college. It told me I was too smart for college. It told me I was headed for greatness, and everything I would touch would turn to gold. That was the story my mind created, not a bad story necessarily, but sometimes a story can work against you. Thinking you are too smart can have both positive and a negative effects. I was short-sighted. My mind told me I should go after success right away, and I listened to it. I didn't know that I had a choice to not listen to my mind. If my mind repeated enough thoughts about the same thing, I would always be inclined to that thing, so instead of going back to college I created a new possibility for myself. I would go out into the world and make myself a success.

• • •

After blowing most of our hot dog money from the summer, I moved to Florida with one of my fraternity brothers. We had five hundred dollars and a small truck between us, and I had paid the first month's rent on a beach house in South Daytona. We didn't have much of a plan other than that we would be the guys who quit college, rode off into the Florida sunset, and made it big. That was the story we created, and our youthful confidence fed it.

After all that had happened, my mind was convinced that just as I was able to grow my hot dog cart into six hot dog carts, I could grow anything into anything. *Something happened*—we were successful with the hot dogs; *I interpreted meaning*—I knew what it took to become successful; and *I made a decision about myself*—I was a successful entrepreneur who could do anything. Just like deciding I was smart because Mrs. Kostyra placed me in the advanced classes, I made a subconscious decision about myself.

• • •

We drove down to Florida. We moved into our house on the beach, and there we were. I expected it to be some kind of magical experience in which incredible opportunities suddenly presented themselves, and we would make it big in business.

After buying some groceries and getting settled, the realization hit us that the next month's rent and utility bills would be due in just a few weeks, and our funds would be depleted in just a few days. I had no desire to just turn around after a few weeks and go back to New Jersey a failure. So we decided to get jobs until we could figure out how to start a business.

My story persisted: Somehow, we were destined for greatness, and as long as I believed it, the reality around me would shape itself in that direction. My buddy's name was John, but everyone including me called him Burger. Burger quit college with me, had worked for Dave and me during the hot dog summers, and knew I had big dreams.

Our Dual Consciousness

He shared those dreams and decided to take a shot with me—and Burger had skills that I didn't have. He knew construction. He knew how to build things, and he brought all his tools with him on our truck.

Dave, my hot dog partner, had stayed in New Jersey to finish college. He was two years older than me, and his parents would never forgive him if he dropped out one semester from graduation. He vowed to come down when he was done to take part in whatever we decided to start, as if it were a certainty. Yet all we had were stories and dreams, and nothing else.

Searching for jobs was difficult because we were in a strange town in a strange state and we didn't know anyone. Burger wanted us to get construction jobs, but we didn't have the money to buy the kinds of tools they needed us to have to get started. But we were enthusiastic, and I knew how to keep knocking on doors until I got what I wanted, so I got us a job as telemarketers selling magazine subscriptions over the phone. Burger didn't like that, and his mind told me through his lips that he didn't leave his girlfriend in New Jersey and quit college to take some stupid job as a telemarketer. So he refused to report for work our first morning on the job, and I drove off in the truck alone.

Now some people say they never forget the defining moments in their lives, and I had an experience that morning that I will never forget. I was driving to my new job. I didn't want to go, either—I didn't quit college and move thirteen hundred miles away from home to take some stupid telemarketing job. During the ride, all the things that had happened to me flashed through my mind, the years selling newspapers and living in the apartment with my brother, the whirlwind of fun times in the college dorms, the incredible success of our little hot dog company. The possibility came into my mind strongly—I was going to do big things, I was *going to do big things*. Then the song "Take It to the Limit" by the Eagles came on the radio. I know it might sound silly, but that song spoke to me, just as songs are designed to do. I interpreted the circumstances of that moment to mean that I wasn't supposed to be going to that silly job. I made a decision right then and there that we were going to start our business right away. I would borrow money if I had to, and I wasn't going to waste time working at some crappy job until I had it. I was so excited about my idea that I drove right past the office I was going to, and went straight home to tell Burger.

• • •

I told Burger the good news. I was all excited. I told him my crude plan: "Tomorrow we will find a store for rent on the boardwalk in Daytona Beach, and open something that would cater to all the people who supposedly come down here for the Daytona 500, Biker Week, and spring break." I brainstormed that we would sell some kind of food, maybe hot dogs again. We could borrow money from his parents. I could ask my uncle for money, too. My mother's sister always had a heart for me, and her husband had money. And we could get Dave to borrow money from his parents, and when he finished school in three months, we would have built the business and he would come in with us.

Then I remembered the six hot dog carts that Dave had stored in his parents' basement. We would have Dave sell those and use that money, too. It was a rough plan, but all of a sudden I had a way of accumulating a bunch of money. If everyone agreed, we could probably raise a lot. And believe it or not, we did. Burger borrowed $2,500 from his dad. I found out that I had relatives that were actually willing to take a chance on me. They knew what I had done throughout high school and with the hot dog carts, so my grandfather and my uncle gave me $2,500. Dave sold the carts for another five grand, and he borrowed three more from his parents under the premise that Burger and I would build the store, whatever it was, and he would join us in a few months. Quickly, we had raised $13,000 to fund our business.

We found a store for rent on the main part of what they called the Strip, right by the boardwalk and the beach. The store used to be a little pizzeria, but it had been gutted. The only thing that remained from the old pizza place was an ice machine that still worked in the back. There was also a sign above the store that said, "Pizza and Subs," so we figured we didn't need to buy a new sign and the landlord said we could use the ice machine, so of course we would just open up a pizzeria. Not that we had any idea of how to do that, but that detail didn't matter. We paid our first month's rent and security deposit to our new landlord, Karl.

Karl owned seven t-shirt shops all called The Rat's Hole. They sold t-shirts with airbrushed slogans to tourists, and Karl obviously did very well for himself. One of his stores was right next to ours, and he said he needed this place to be open again so he would have a place to eat lunch every day. He also organized the events that took place during the annual Bike Week, when motorcycle guys from all over the country came to Daytona. Karl was known in town and nationally by all the bikers as Big Daddy Rat, and he was our landlord.

Burger and I spent the next few months building the pizzeria. We knew we needed tables and chairs and booths and countertops and things like that. We knew we would need pizza ovens and a sandwich area and a cash register. Even though we had no idea how to make pizza, we figured we would also need a mixer for the dough, and we were happy that we already had an ice machine. We made it up in our heads as we went along, deciding what we needed based on our notion of what a pizzeria was. We bought what we could from the restaurant supply store, and we listened to advice from all the locals.

We made a lot of mistakes. We bought a thousand-dollar oven that was electric instead of gas, and we couldn't hook it up without changing the kind of electricity that went into the building. What the hell

Our Dual Consciousness

did we know? We tried to make our money stretch. We bought what we had to, and Burger built the countertops, tables, and pizza work area. He put the floors in and hung a drop ceiling.

After we were about halfway done building the place, we ran out of money. We still needed a walk-in refrigerator, chairs, lighting, and a whole bunch of other things. We needed to keep paying the rent on the store and our house. We needed start-up money for the food we were going to prepare, even though we still had no idea how to make pizza, and we needed food ourselves to live on. We were broke, and unless we got more money, we would be done with this project before it ever really began.

Dave finished school and came down to join the fun. He and Burger kept working on the place, and it was my job to somehow get us more money. Dave and Burger had Dave's car now, so I drove back to New Jersey in the truck on a mission to beg, borrow or steal. People were enthralled with our story, but very few were interested in lending us ten thousand dollars to finish and open the store. I had to knock on a lot of doors, but finally I convinced one of our frat brothers to shell out the rest of the cash. Ricky came from money, and he also knew what we had done with the hot dog carts. I told him he would be a full partner, and we would pay him back. Ricky trusted me, so now we had four partners—three working ones and one silent.

• • •

It took us three months to build the pizzeria. We called it "The Pizza Guys," and we had one of Big Daddy Rat's air-brushers paint a huge mural across the front wall with a picture of our four partners. The pizza place looked incredible. We couldn't believe we had actually built it and were ready to open. Now we had to learn how to make pizza and everything else we needed to prepare and sell. Dave got some meatball and sauce recipes from his mother, and we decided what kind of sub sandwiches to sell. We practiced making and mixing the dough in the huge mixer we bought.

We called a few pizzerias in New Jersey and asked how to make pizza. They thought we were crazy, but we were serious. We figured it out, and after a while the pizzas started coming out round. We practiced cooking and making everything for a few days. We developed a system for taking orders, preparing the food, clearing off tables, getting everything prepped, and getting everything cleaned and ready for the next day. We were open just in time for the Daytona 500 crowd. After a few weeks of getting customers, we got the hang of it.

Our Dual Consciousness

Burger, Dave, and me with a bunch of our fraternity brothers who came down to visit us during spring break, 1987. Not pictured to the left is the airbrushed portrait of Ricky, our silent partner who was not available when the mural was done. We didn't have a picture of him, either, so I just described him to the artist. His mural looked nothing like him.

Karl Smith, Big Daddy Rat, and his famous, "Rat's Hole."

• • •

We had done it. We created a possibility about how we would do it, and now we were actually in business. People say to be careful what you wish for because you just might get it.

Working the pizza place was not as easy as working the hot dog carts. It wasn't as fun, either. And, sure, we had each other, but our families and everyone else we knew well were in New Jersey. We had to be at the store by 9 a.m. to get the ovens started and get the food ready. Like the Jersey Shore, people would want to eat after the bars closed, so usually we didn't close until 3 a.m. It took all three of us to handle the crowds, so our hours were horrendous. We would go home at night and have to wake up a few hours later and then go back to work.

We had thought we were riding into the Florida sunset, but it was not like that at all. We never went to the beach. We never left the pizza place. Our first week we served the Daytona 500 crowd, and we did pretty well. A few weeks later was Bike Week, and we did amazingly well. Since we were next to The Rat's Hole, our store was packed with bikers for the entire week. We stayed open till 5 a.m. every day during Bike Week, and we even hired some locals to help us. We made twenty thousand dollars that week, and we thought business would stay like that forever.

Bike Week turned out to be the biggest week we would ever have. After that we worked through several weeks of spring breaks, as different colleges

Our Dual Consciousness

came down at different times. We did well those weeks, too, but after that, business died off.

We were all young. Burger and I were twenty-one, and we missed our days living in the dorms and partying with our frat brothers. Having four partners was a big problem. We would all take what we needed out of the cash register, and we had a bad system for budgeting our money. We were working all the time. We were exhausted. Our minds started to clash, because we each had our own story about how things should be, and we started fighting all the time.

• • •

We were able to build our business because we created a story about how great the pizzeria would be. The sense of possibility central to that story allowed us to achieve our goals. Our minds created positive stories about what we were doing. But our minds were just as capable of creating negative stories. In fact, our minds were even *better* at creating negative stories. That's what the mind does—it finds problems. It loves to find problems. We let our minds run wild. We let our minds control us. It was so easy to do, and we had no idea it was happening. We were like rats in a cage, letting the natural habits of the mind take their toll on us.

It was not the situation itself that led to our downfall. It was the stories we were creating in our minds. We could have created new stories about how we could continue to succeed, but we didn't. We didn't know we could create new stories. We were blind to the fact that we owed our success to the stories we had created, and the possibilities that came with them. We believed our thoughts were real. We believed that our stories about each other and our situation were real. We couldn't distinguish between thoughts and reality. If we had, we might have recognized what we were doing, and changed course.

But it was a big drama now. A drama we had created in our heads. It would have been great to realize at the time that we were young and free with little responsibility. We had a world of possibility at our feet. We could have been happy and enjoyed our lives. But we didn't, because we were trapped in a mind-created story that said our life was now a big problem.

The choice to change course was absent for one simple reason: We didn't know we had a choice. We didn't know that we could look at the situation and choose to not fight about it. We didn't know that we could look at what was happening, see how we were interpreting it, and choose what decisions we would make. We let our minds choose for us.

I learned a lot about fighting with people I care about through this experience. We were best friends—Dave, Burger, and me. We were fraternity brothers in college, and we lived like brothers out of college. We shared each other's stuff, and we shared a common goal. But the work got to us. Seven days a week with only a few hours off at a time was not ideal. We couldn't imagine the idea of continuing to work from 9 a.m. to at least midnight every single

Our Dual Consciousness

day. Sometimes this is what it takes to make it in the restaurant business, but that life was not for us. We were making enough money to stay in business, but splitting the pot four ways every week, was not going to make us rich—or at least that is the story we created.

Our fights remind me of the fights married couples have during financial difficulties. Dave would say how our main problem was that we had no system for budgeting our money between us, and we all took money out of the register whenever we wanted. I argued that our main problem was that we weren't giving away free pizzas to all the hotel managers so that they would encourage their guests to order from us. Of course Dave was right, and I was right, too, but we argued constantly about whose ideas were better. Usually I was arguing about one thing, and he was arguing about something completely different. This is what occurs between most couples who get divorced, and we were definitely about to get divorced from each other.

Burger's biggest problem was that he was not comfortable dealing with customers or making pizzas and sandwiches. He kept telling us that he was not cut out for this, and of course, he was also right. He was great at building things, and once we built the place, there was nothing left for him to put his talent into.

We had another problem, too. We never got our lease signed by Big Daddy Rat. We started to have ideas about selling the place—it really was a beautiful pizzeria, fully equipped and ready for any buyer to come in and make a go of it. We thought we might actually be able to sell it, make a profit, and get out. To do this we would need to have a lease that offered an option to continue leasing after the one- or two-year lease period was up, but we didn't have that. We overlooked it during our startup phase.

When we realized this, we asked the Rat to give us our signed lease. He refused and told us we didn't need one. That's when we started asking other business owners that rented from the Rat what they thought. We heard several stories from the other storeowners about how the Rat did business. More than one told us that a few years ago, the Rat and some of his biker buddies broke one his tenant's kneecaps for arguing over a similar matter. Apparently the Rat was like the biker mafia down in Florida.

We didn't know if these rumors were true. We had no way of substantiating them, but that didn't matter. We had enough information to create our own story about what was happening. We decided that the Rat was never going to give us our lease. We also decided, based on how he was acting, that he would wait until we were ready to give up on the business and take it over since he owned the building and the pizza place we had built was part of it now. We based our assumptions on things that he said, but we never knew if they were true or not. We wanted a way out of the situation, and our fears and

Our Dual Consciousness

fantasies about what could happen served to unify us once again.

• • •

We followed what our minds were telling us. In other words, we were following the story we created about the Rat, and how he was going to take over our pizza place and keep our equipment, and we would have done all our hard work for nothing. It is important to point out here again that we did not realize that the story we created was nothing but a story—it was not necessarily what was really happening—but at that point in my life, I did not recognize the ability to look at what was happening and be aware of the story my mind was creating. I assumed that the story I created was my only option. I could have created new possibilities that would have allowed for a different outcome, but I didn't realize I had the power to do that.

The new story we created was that we had to close the pizzeria. We weren't about to let the Rat take us over, so we decided we would take it apart in the middle of the night, put all the equipment on a rented truck, drive it all to Dave's parents' house, store it in their basement, and start working to put it all back together in a new store that we either operated ourselves or tried to sell. We figured things might be different if we were in New Jersey, where pizzerias did well all year round, we had all our other friends around, and we wouldn't be trapped in a fight with each other.

So we rented a truck and hired a few guys from the restaurant supply place to move the heavy equipment. We waited for The Rat's Hole next door to us to close and for Karl to go home for the night. We put newspaper over the front windows, and then we started taking apart the pizza place that took us three months to build. It was not easy. By dawn, we were all exhausted. All of us were bleeding and scratched up. It was a scary night. We all had it in the back of our minds that the Rat would show up with his kneecap-breaking buddies and say, "What do guys think you're doing?" We felt like we were stealing the place. Even though it was all our stuff, it felt like a *Mission Impossible* heist.

We loaded up our truck to the max. We even took the Rat's ice machine. Fuck him. We also took all our furniture from the beach house, filling up every inch of the twenty-two-foot truck.

As we pulled away, we kept waiting for the Rat to see us, but he never showed up. We would always wonder what happened the next day when Karl came to our door for lunch, only to see that The Pizza Guys had vanished into thin air.

• • •

We drove up Route 95 toward New Jersey for about five hours until we thought we were far enough away. We got a hotel room and slept for the rest of the day and the next night. When we got to Dave's house, there were twenty-five of our fraternity brothers there to greet us and help us to unload the truck into the basement. His parents were surprised to see us, and they didn't seem too happy about us putting a pizzeria in their basement.

• • •

I slept at Dave's parents' house for a few days. Burger went home to his parents' house. My mind would tell me that was the difference between my friends and me. My father lived in a little apartment with his wife, and my mother lived in a house in the woods far away from where I grew up. If I was desperate, I could have stayed with one of them, but my mind said that I couldn't. My mind told me not to eat food out of someone else's refrigerator. But mostly, the story I held on to was that I had no one to take care of me, so that meant that I had it harder than everybody else.

This was the biggest part of the story I had created about myself. I remembered living as a child with no food in the house; and my parents fighting constantly, and not having clean clothes to wear to school, and supporting myself through high school. I would see my friend's parents cooking for them and doing their laundry, and I couldn't help but get mad, because I never had that. I would get mad because I knew that I had earned so much money already in my life and most of it was used to pay bills, whereas I had friends who were able to live at home and use their money to buy whatever they wanted. This story stayed with me always. I thought about this all throughout my college years, down the shore during the hot dog summers, and in Florida. It kept me constantly upset underneath the persona that showed to the world.

Chapter 4
The Child Is the Father of the Man

It is never obvious that stories you created in your youth continue to drive your future actions. I was back in New Jersey. I was broke. I had no car and no place to live. My brother had pledged the same fraternity as I had, so he was now my fraternity brother as well as my real brother. I moved into his dorm room for the last few weeks of the semester.

It was great not having to work sixteen hours a days in the pizza place, and I enjoyed the vacation at college. School was ending though, and my brother, like me, had no home to go to during the summers. He planned to stay with our aunt, so I came along with him. I felt like a failure, but I had to live somewhere. We never did start up talk about taking the equipment from the pizza place and building another store. None of us had any money to get started, and we decided to sell everything. We used the money to pay off our loans. We still owed Ricky $6,000, so Burger, Dave, and me took turns making Ricky's car payment for a few years. Eventually we decided we were square.

• • •

I was determined to become self-sufficient as soon as possible. I got a job delivering pizza during the lunch shift at a place around the corner. They had their own delivery trucks, so I didn't need a car. With tips, the pay was pretty good, about seventy-five bucks for a three-and-a-half-hour shift. I earned enough to buy a piece-of-crap car. I ran across my old boss from when I sold newspaper subscriptions years earlier, and he gave me a good idea. Jimmy Botbyle ran crews of kid salesmen that canvassed neighborhoods for subscriptions to the *Herald News*. When I saw Jimmy, he explained how he had to give up the business because he had a bad case of diabetes and wound up losing one of his feet. He couldn't drive anymore, so now he was a toll collector on the Garden State Parkway taking quarters from people. But he told me he had paid his kids five dollars a sale, as he had done for me years ago. I knew he got more than we did, but I didn't realize how much more. Jimmy told me he used to get $23 for each subscription. Jimmy did that for over twenty years and managed to set himself up pretty well.

    I decided to get myself a contract with a newspaper. I didn't want to run a crew of kids, though. I made up the possibility of going out in the afternoons, knocking on doors as I used to, and getting all the sales myself, but this time at a much higher commission. I still looked pretty young, and instead of telling the customers I was trying to win a ten-speed bike, I would tell them I was trying to win a college scholarship.

The Child Is the Father of the Man

The *Star Ledger*, a local New Jersey newspaper, was very receptive to my request. I told them of my success years earlier with Jimmy Botbyle, and they gave me a contract under which I would get $25 for every new subscription. Whenever I tell this story, someone always asks why they would pay so much, so I always explain that newspapers make their money from advertising, not from subscription sales. Circulation numbers are all that matter to their advertisers, so the newspaper will pay a lot to have a steady stream of new subscriptions. I went out from 4 to 7 p.m. every day after delivering pizza. I also went out on Saturday mornings. I averaged eight sales a day. The *Star Ledger* thought I had a little crew of my own because I brought them fifty new subscriptions every week, but I got them all myself, and at $25 bucks a sale, I was hauling in a nice bundle. Soon I didn't even need to deliver pizza anymore. After taxes, I was taking in a thousand a week, working only three hours a day.

I was proud of myself for creating a profitable business that required so little effort. I realized how silly it was to work a regular job when I could just invent my own way to make money. I bought a brand new car, got a nice apartment, and acquired everything else I needed to become a productive citizen again.

• • •

I knew I couldn't do this forever. I had no interest in hiring kids and driving them around, but I would eventually start looking too old to get away with the help-me-to-get-a-college-scholarship bullshit. I also had some problems with what my mind was telling me. It told me that I was ultimately a failure in business. It told me that if I had stayed in college, I would have graduated by now, and then I might have been able to find a real job with a real future. It told me that after all I've been through, here I am again walking the streets and selling newspapers.

• • •

My brother moved into my apartment after he quit college, and the two of us had lots of fun going out to bars, meeting girls, skiing in the winter, going down the shore in the summer, and living the bachelor life. It was great, and I was able to pay the bills, but I still had a story in my mind that I was *supposed* to be achieving bigger things, because I was *capable* of doing so. From this positive story, which I was lucky enough to always have with me, I created the possibility of doing more with my life.

I went to an employment agency to see what kinds of jobs were available for a guy like me—someone who dropped out of college and had experience in running three different businesses. It turned out that companies weren't really too interested in hiring people who thought they were entrepreneurs. My resume was not too impressive. There seemed to be a very fine line between what one might consider an entrepreneur and what one might consider a total screw-up who has jumped in and out of business. The owner of the employment agency liked my story, though, so he hired me to work directly for the agency. I took the job as a personnel consultant, also known as a headhunter.

My job was to find employees for companies. Companies would pay fees to employment agencies for finding qualified candidates that met their exact specifications. The fees were big. The agency I was working for placed mostly secretaries, so if I found a secretary that got hired at $30,000 a year, the fee would be one percent per thousand dollars, or 30 percent in this case: $9,000. Of that, my commission would be 40 percent. Not bad for a couple of phone calls. I don't know who invented this business, but a lot of people were doing it, and they were making a lot of money. They gave me a cold call list, and I would call companies that paid agencies for this service, and asked them if they needed secretaries. If they gave me what was called a job order, I would cold call secretaries asking them if they wanted to change jobs—essentially, I was stealing secretaries from one company and placing them into a new company. I was hunting for heads.

• • •

I spent every day hunting for job orders and people to fill them. I learned the lingo and put together a good little speech for every situation. It felt like I was doing something that had more potential than knocking on doors, even though I still did that every night until I made money in my new office job. I would wear a suit and a tie, and I had a shared secretary who would even bring me coffee. This job promised an impressive future, and I was good at doing it. It wasn't much different from knocking on doors and selling newspaper subscriptions. I made more phone calls than everyone else in the office, and had a knack for talking people into doing what I wanted—companies gave me their job orders. I also knew a lot of young women who were looking for work.

I was only twenty-three, and my friends had friends, too. I went to bars, and instead of just looking for girls to date, I was looking for girls to place into jobs, and they were everywhere. Every woman I met would be either a potential date or a potential job candidate. It was a win–win situation for a young guy like me. I built up a network of people that was unmatched in the little agency I worked in. After one year, I was the top salesperson in the office. I broke every record they ever had, and out of one hundred and fifty offices the company had nationwide, I was ranked twenty-second in the country. They even put my picture in the company's monthly magazine centerfold.

I used my skills to put myself in a comfortable position with the company, but then my story about myself intervened. I started realizing how much money my boss, the owner of this branch of the company, was making. I was getting a 40 percent commission, but he was getting the other 60 percent. I started trying to figure out what kind of story this guy created to put himself in the position where he was getting a 60 percent commission on all of my sales. I started calculating how much it would cost to rent my own office space and get my own phones. Of course my mind was afraid of making a change, because the mind always finds something negative to worry about, but my one positive story about myself was bigger than any negative story my mind could create. I was smart. Mrs. Kostyra let me know it years ago, and I still believed it. I was definitely smarter than that putz who ran the agency and called himself my boss, so I created a brand new possibility for myself. I was going to open my own employment agency.

• • •

At this point in my life, I was no role model. I only cared about myself. I didn't fully realize that a world existed outside of myself. I thought my story was the most fascinating story in the world, and ignored everyone else's. I had no responsibility other than fulfilling my own wants and needs, so I drank almost every night with my frat brothers. I went on a million first dates. A relationship was the last thing on my mind. I looked at woman as just another way of enhancing the image I had of myself as an up-and-coming entrepreneur. You might even say that I had very little integrity, for I would make any move necessary to enhance my own interests in life and in business without consideration of the people I was affecting.

I spent a few weeks stealing all the files in the office. I copied every single job order my agency had ever written. I copied the resumes of every applicant who was currently looking for work. I stole every lead that I could get my hands on, and then I quit. I rented office space a few miles away. It was my own little building with its own parking lot. There was a big office for me, and three smaller ones for more consultants. I even had a big waiting room with an area for a receptionist and a place to test typing skills for the potential secretarial candidates. My plan was to recreate the exact same situation I had come from but this time, I would make 100 percent of my own commissions and 60 percent of everyone else's.

I had also done splits with other agencies, meaning they or I would provide either the candidate or the job order and the two agencies would split the commissions. This is not unlike what realtors do when one realtor has the buyer and one has the seller. Since I had done so much business at the other office, I already knew many of the other small agency owners like mine, and they were perfectly willing to do business with me. This would allow me to fill any new order I could get by simply farming them out to other agencies if I had to. I would make more now on splits, too, because I was getting the full commission. I bought desks, chairs, word processors, typewriters, business cards, a phone system, and fax and copy machines. I was in business.

• • •

My business looked impressive to everyone I knew. My office had a giant desk with a big leather chair, and I hung all my plaques and awards on the wall behind my desk. My mind created an image of myself: I was a real big shot. I was a real egomaniac and it showed.

I hired a receptionist. I trained three other consultants to work for me, and everyone was making money. I figured out many immensely helpful things about sales. I was relentless in finding new clients. I knew that the more calls I made, the more new sales possibilities I would create. I also learned that it was possible to turn anyone into a customer. I would call certain companies every single day until I got the person I wanted. I wouldn't take no for an answer, because no was usually the first answer I would ever get. Most people interpreted no to mean they couldn't do business with that person. Something would happen—the client would say no. The salesperson would interpret meaning from that—the client doesn't want to do business. The salesperson would make a decision based on that interpretation—their business cannot be gotten. But unlike this hypothetical salesperson, I knew how to create new possibilities, even though I wasn't conscious of this knowledge or what I was doing with it.

For example, I called a customer, a human resources manager at a company that paid fees to agencies. I called her every day for two months and she would not take my call. I knew she did business with the other agencies, but she probably didn't want to take on any more, and I was probably such a pain in the ass that she refused to take my call on principle. After two months, she finally told her secretary to tell me that she wasn't working with any new agencies. At that point, most people would create a story that said that they were never going to be able to do business with her. I looked at the situation carefully. Why wouldn't she do business with me? She didn't even know me. I tried to picture how my calling every day looked to her; probably pretty annoying. I pictured in my mind how she would react when her secretary would say, "It's that pain in the ass agent again." Her name was Onalise. I knew she had a ton of business to give, and I wanted it. I thought of a new possibility that would win her over. I had one of my buddies, who was an art major in college, draw me a cartoon comic strip with six panels on it. The first panel had a cartoon picture of me calling and asking for Onalise. The second and third panel showed her secretary saying I was on the phone and Onalise saying, "Tell him I'm not here." The final three panels showed me saying, "OK, I'll call back tomorrow," and her saying, "What a pain in the ass!!" The comic strip was pretty funny, and she must have laughed her head off after I faxed it into her office, because she called me in to meet her the very next day.

Over the next year, I did over a hundred thousand dollars in business with Onalise. I didn't accept the negative story that my mind created automatically, which said, "You can't get this one." Instead I created a new plan that gave me a possibility for success. I did this often, and sometimes it worked and sometimes it didn't, but I learned that it was possible to create new approaches to create new possibilities. The agency did well for years.

• • •

My agency was called Corporate Search Associates. My dream was to become as big as the biggest agency in New Jersey, Executive Search Associates. They had seven offices, and I thought it would be just a matter of time before I caught them. I had four consultants working for me, and it would be easy to open another office and have one of my consultants manage that one. I could even manage it myself and bounce back and forth between the two places. I started creating a plan for how I would make that happen, but then something else started happening. It was called the recession of 1989.

Business slowed down. Apparently, I had been working through a period in the staffing industry that was considered a boom, but that boom was ending. During this recession, jobs became scarce. When there are fewer jobs being offered, job candidates send resumes directly to companies, flooding them with potential new hires. Many of my client companies decided that they didn't need to use agencies any more.

The consultants who worked for me couldn't make placements anymore, and slowly they owed me more on their draws than they were making on commissions. One by one my consultants disappeared. Everyone in the business started talking about how tough things were getting. A story in my mind was growing stronger: The employment business was disappearing. I had made enough money to stay in business for a long time, so I toughed it out for another year and a half. Finally, Executive Search closed five of its seven offices. That was all it took for me to justify my decision to close mine.

I didn't know at the time that I could have created a new story, one that offered the possibility for surviving the tough years or changing my business in some way so that it would make money again. I just followed the natural path that my mind laid out for me. Some things happened—the recession, and Executive Search closing five of their offices. I interpreted meaning—the industry was disappearing, and companies were not going to use agencies anymore. I made a decision based on my interpretation—I should go out of business and do something else. So I closed my business, again.

• • •

I always thought I was doing the right thing. I thought I was too smart to stay in a sinking boat, and I justified my actions by planning to move on to the next thing. It was always so easy to create a story about why I should go out of business. I had already done it several times. I was always so good at creating new possibilities that allowed me to open up new businesses, but I was never very good at recognizing the negative stories that would prompt me to go out of business. I never considered the idea that I was responsible for the downfall of my businesses. I blamed external forces, and to a certain extent they were responsible, but I never chose to explore the possibility of staying in business.

By the time I was twenty-six years old I had already gone out of business three times. My mind created a negative story that I was a failure in business, but it also created a positive story that I was still an entrepreneur because I had created so much at such a young age, and was still capable of creating more.

My mind hung on to the story that I was neglected as a child, that I had it harder than anyone else, that I had a bad start in life. When my mind told me to be mad, things that happened in the past would bother me now. Even though there was nothing I could do to address any of those past problems, my mind put petty thoughts in my head all the time. I defined myself by my stories. I thought I was a series of events. I didn't understand that those things I had done were not really who I was. But I continued to walk around, unaware, for a little while longer.

I continued to do what felt good. I had some money saved up, but I didn't want to blow it, so I took an easy job selling over-the-counter pharmaceuticals to pharmacies in supermarkets. It was the kind of job that put me on the road every day, and I never saw a boss. My instructions were given through voicemail messages. I liked that, so I kept the job. I drank almost every night, and for a while, I lived to do nothing but have fun.

I lived in the apartment with my brother. Our place became like a frat house for frat boys that were too old for college. It was fun for a while, but it didn't take long for me to start questioning where I was going in my life. I started to see a lot of my friends taking on real careers that I had locked myself out of because I never graduated from college. For some reason, I was still mad at my parents. That never went away. I still blamed them for my having such a bad start in life. Ultimately, in my mind, any undesirable circumstances in my life were the fault of my parents. I had it hard because they didn't take care of me. I quit college because they did not provide me with the proper guidance or home life. If I could have lived at home all these years like all of my friends, I would have saved up a fortune. My mind held on to those thoughts, and it held on to the anger that those thoughts would produce.

It sounds so silly now, but those silly thoughts were keeping me from growing up. My attitude was the same as it was when I was young. I was trying to prove I could make it without my parents, as if I still needed to prove that. I was older now, but in my mind I was still a fifteen-year-old kid who needed to prove something. I was so wrapped up in the idea that money would make me happy. Everything I saw became a vehicle for me to succeed, as if I knew what it meant to succeed. People interested me only if I could see a way for them to enhance my own success.

I was run by my mind. My mind would help me get money and social status, and it was there to protect me. My mind didn't care about anyone else but me. Anyone who had a better job or more money than I was a threat to my mind. My mind was an egomaniac. It had to be the best, or else it felt threatened. My mind was always uncomfortable around anyone whom it considered more important, more successful, or somehow better than the person I thought I was. My mind, like most minds, had an inferiority complex and justified why I was as good or better than everyone else.

• • •

Meanwhile, my parents were doing well with their lives. My father was working a steady job, and he was harnessing his talent for creating beautiful pencil drawings. He was selling his drawings at local art shows, and he had learned to frame his own work. He even did framing on the side for local art galleries. My father and Karen had a daughter of their own, and he was a good father to her. When I get mad at how he used to be, I have to remember that I am not mad at my father—I am mad at the things that were done by a younger, immature version of the man who is there now.

My mother was working for her husband Gabe, running his insurance agency. They were doing very well with their business, and they also had a large income through the apartment complex they owned. Keith and I always had a story about my mother—that she should be helping us. My mother and her husband were millionaires, and they would fly all over the world often for vacation. They drove fancy cars and lived in a five-thousand-square-foot house set on fifty acres of land. Of course we knew that their money was obtained by Gabe and his good business sense, but when my mother would brag about how well she was doing and what she was buying, our story always answered, "Hello, don't you see that we're still struggling here?"

My mother, although she was not really responsible for many of the stories we created about her, would never acknowledge that we had a difficult childhood. By acknowledging it, she probably would have had to make herself wrong. She had her own story of struggle back then, and I've heard her tell it a million times; how she had to work to get her own apartment, hold two jobs, and support her kids. Her story of struggle lasted for about five years, and then she became the wife of a rich man. Keith and I resented her success because we felt that our own story of struggle was never-ending.

Chapter 5
Awakening from the Mind-created Story

Relationships were difficult. My mind told me that I needed to keep looking for the perfect woman, a woman who would enhance me and my ego, a woman whom I could add to myself like a line to my resume.

My routine for meeting new women was a lot like my sales routine. I was a good talker, and I had good stories to tell. I met a lot of new women, but our relationships never lasted very long. Once I got a girl to like me, it felt like I had closed the sale, and my job was done. In other words, trying to meet women felt like another job. I went out to bars almost every night and went on a million first dates.

But I was getting tired of the same old routine. There had to be more to live for than getting drunk with my buddies and chasing girls. One night at a bar, I tapped a girl on the shoulder and asked her to be my date. I knew right away that this girl was different, because as crazy as it sounds, when I walked around that night holding her hand, I felt like I had been holding her hand for my entire life. Our hands were a perfect fit. Cathy didn't believe anything I told her. She challenged everything I said that night, and continues to challenge me every day. We grew up in the same exact area of New Jersey, but had never met. We found that we lived just a few blocks from each other.

I called her the next morning, but nobody picked up the phone. She lived with her sister and brother-in-law, who were apparently having some sort of a problem with a raccoon living in their attic. When her sister finally noticed the unfamiliar number on her caller ID, she called it back and said, "Is this the raccoon guy?"

I played along. "Yes, this is the raccoon guy. What seems to be the problem?"

After her sister figured out that I was some guy Cathy had met in the bar the night before, Cathy and I started talking and we never stopped.

• • •

Cathy was an Italian Jersey girl. She grew up in a household with tough Italian guys, and women who prepared and cooked their own spaghetti sauce every Sunday. (They don't call it sauce, though, and will always point out that it is called gravy.) I was a Jew—at least that is what I was told as a kid. I was not a big, tough, Italian guy, but I sounded tough over the phone.

Normally a girl like Cathy, who came from that type of family, would not have been my preference. But Cathy was not like the superficial, North Jersey Italian girls I had known in the past. She was funny and knew how to have a good time. She laughed at all my stupid jokes, and she tolerated the messy apartment that I shared with my brother. We just fit. We were comfortable with each other, and spent all our time together. We did boyfriend and girlfriend things like go to the park and push each other on the swings. We flew kites and did all the cliché stuff you see in movies. It was so easy for us to become a couple that even my friends told me that I was definitely going to marry this girl.

• • •

I loved her. Now since I have been distinguishing between what is real and what is a story, and since this question come up in talks, I will pose the question to you: Is the statement, "I loved her," a story?

Something happened—I met a girl, was attracted to her, and needed to be with her every day. She was someone I had to talk to before I went to bed every night, and someone with whom I had to share everything that happened to me during the day. I interpreted meaning—I couldn't be without her, and we would enhance each other's lives by being together. I made a decision—I loved her. Now, maybe this actually is a just a story, but like any other big story I have ever created, it felt and still feels completely real.

• • •

Cathy had her own past and current problems to grapple with. On our second date I learned that Cathy's mother had passed away just three months before I met her. I joked that her mother sent me to her to protect her. Even though it was just something I would say, my mind adopted that story as if it were an absolute fact.

Cathy's parents, like mine, had been divorced since she was a kid. Philomena had gone deaf at age thirty-eight, the year Cathy was born. After the divorce, Philomena took care of Cathy, the baby of the family. Having gone deaf at such a late age, Philomena learned how to read lips, but there were no one's lips she knew how to read better than Cathy's. Cathy spent her childhood speaking with mother constantly, but not always needing to add voice to the movements of her lips. Even after we were married for many years, every once in a while Cathy mouthed her words to me, expecting me to understand what she was saying.

It was later discovered that Philomena developed small tumors in her ears as a result of a condition called Von Hippel Lindau or VHL. VHL causes cysts and tumors to manifest in the organs of the body. Generally VHL tumors are found in patients' kidneys, pancreas, eyes, ears, spinal column, and the bottom of the brain in the cerebellum. Patients with VHL may find they have tumors in some or all of these areas, and if they are found early and checked regularly, surgeries can usually remove them before they cause life-threatening problems. The condition was discovered in Philomena when she was in her mid-fifties. It was already too late to repair her hearing, and they found other problems as well. She had multiple tumors in her kidneys, and had both removed. On dialysis for the rest of her life, she and Cathy moved in with her other daughter, Annette.

As I said, Cathy's mother passed away three months before I met Cathy, but when our relationship started, Cathy knew she had a big secret to share. She told me about her family history, and she told me what had already happened to her—she had inherited her mother's condition. VHL had been passed down in Cathy's family for generations, affecting her grandmother, uncle, mother, and brother, whose spinal tumors led to paralysis and eventually a botched operation that caused his death at eighteen. That operation took place in 1965, long before VHL was ever diagnosed, and with the less advanced surgical techniques of the time. Cathy's elder sister, Stella, had tumors in almost all the places that they generally manifest. Family members argue that she probably should have been treated earlier and more frequently for the disease, but reluctant to deal with it, Stella passed away at the age of forty-two.

Cathy's mother had four other siblings and they all had big families of their own so VHL symptoms had been popping up for years throughout the family. Her cousin Frankie was the first to take action toward identifying the family members who were affected. Frankie was a rough and tough Italian boy from North Jersey. He got into fights, experimented with drugs, and had more than a few wild nights drinking in bars. One night he got into a fight that resulted in him getting hit in the face with a pipe. After losing one of his eyes as a result, the doctors noticed that his other eye only had partial vision. The loss of vision in his remaining eye was caused by multiple, microscopic tumors. After further investigation at the hands of many different doctors, tumors were found in Frankie's brain, spinal column, and kidneys. He underwent many surgeries over many years. Tumors in his cerebellum were removed affecting his speech and balance. There were so many tumors in his kidneys that one kidney was completely removed and the other one was reduced after surgery to just a fraction of its original size.

Frankie was asked to participate in a study offered by the National Institute of Health (NIH) in Bethesda, Maryland. There they were studying families from all over the world and developing protocols and treatments. Frankie, after his many afflictions, had become a religious man. He even wound up participating in several human aid endeavors sponsored by the Peace Corps, and he spent his remaining strong years helping those less fortunate in this world. Frankie was identified as a carrier of VHL in his mid-thirties, and he knew that if he had been treated earlier, several of his afflictions could have been prevented. It was Frankie who insisted that everyone in his family be tested for VHL so that they could be treated as early in their life as possible.

So, at Frankie's insistence, Cathy, Annette, and two of Frankie's sisters flew down to the NIH in Bethesda. The four women received MRIs, CAT scans, and ultrasounds for an entire week. Doctors checked their eyes, ears, kidneys, pancreases, spinal columns, and brains for any signs of cysts or tumors. When it was all said and done, three of the four showed no signs of the disease. Cathy, the youngest of the group at only twenty years old, knew they saw something when they requested that she stay longer for several of the scans. She was the only one on the trip who received a diagnosis.

As she explained all this to me, her mind brought back the memories and the emotions that came along with the news. In the following months, Cathy had several laser surgeries to remove small tumors from her eyes. She didn't realize it at the time, but she had already lost some vision in her left eye. Doctors were able to neutralize the problem, though, and felt they could now control it as long as she had her eyes checked and treated regularly. They also took the preventative measures of removing a kidney tumor and a small spinal tumor. Again, they left her confident that as long as she got regular scans, they would be able to keep her condition in check. Because Cathy was one of the youngest patients to ever be diagnosed, we were optimistic that she would live a normal, healthy, and productive life. You might say that this was the possibility we created, and it was a pretty good one.

• • •

Cathy's father is Ernie. He looks exactly like John Gotti, the famed mob boss, and was very protective of his youngest daughter. I was a fast-talking, wise-ass, punk that was taking his daughter from him. I was not Italian, and I don't think Ernie had ever even met a Jew in his entire life. He didn't trust me. I had very little money. I didn't know how to do any kind of construction. All I had were stories of businesses I had opened, and I don't think he believed a word of it. In his eyes, I was all talk, and I was a risky prospect for his daughter.

I didn't understand him at the time. I didn't understand why he seemed so grim and worried all the time. I didn't understand what it was like to be him—to have lived through his experiences. I only understood how things were for me. My mind didn't allow me to understand what it would be like to have once watched his eighteen-year-old son become paralyzed and die. My mind wouldn't let me understand what it was like to be so worried about his other child, who carried the same disease.

Cathy and I were opposites in many ways. I was an obnoxious, arrogant asshole, whom most people knew had no moral values or integrity, especially with women and business. She was a sweet, well-spoken, pleasant person who was always smiling. We understood each other. We knew that our relationship was based on more than just superficial interests. We could tell each other anything, and we respected each other's feelings. I had no interest in being with anyone else. I had finally found someone who made me feel that way. Cathy and I examined our life situations carefully, and we discussed the idea of getting married a lot.

Awakening from the Mind-created Story

It was around this time when I had a major breakthrough in my perspective on life, and began to look at how I was operating in a new way. My mother, whom I have not really characterized so far in this story, had been involved in a certain organization since the seventies. The organization was called Erhard Seminar Training. It was commonly known as the EST training. EST, founded by Werner H. Erhard, was a two-weekend, sixty-hour course. The purpose of EST was "to transform one's ability to experience living so that the situations one had been trying to change or had been putting up with, clear up just in the process of life itself."

The EST training was offered from late 1971 to late 1984. I actually took this course when I was only thirteen, at my parents' insistence. The course itself discussed many of the ideas that I have been expressing throughout my story so far, such as the idea of identifying what is real in your life and what is a story. I have not credited myself as the "enlightened person" the course claims it creates. The reason I have not given myself this label is because I had been too young to have created very many deep-rooted stories, or at least had not identified them yet. The experience of the course seemed lost on me. I even created stories for myself that said my mother spent so much time indulging herself in EST seminars and trying to "find herself" that she completely ignored what was happening to me as a child and a young adult. One might argue, however, that my ability to overcome challenges as a young adult may be credited to the intrinsic knowledge I obtained from that course as a child.

When I met Cathy, my mother was still very involved in this work. EST later became an organization called the Landmark Forum. Its principles remained the same, but had been polished and improved over the years. As it described itself, it brought about "positive and permanent shifts in the quality of your life. These shifts are the direct cause for a new and unique kind of freedom and power—the freedom to be absolutely at ease no matter what the circumstance, the power to be in action effectively in those areas that are important to you."

Cathy and I took the course at my mother's urging. There I was able to identify many of the big stories I had held on to throughout my life. I was able to see what drove me to make many of the decisions I had. I realized how I held so much anger toward my parents, and that they had been just two young people who were trying to figure out their own lives. I was able to see that they never meant to hurt me in any way, and that my interpretation of what happened to me was only that, an interpretation. I was able to forgive them, finally. I was also able to see how I was driven by an urge to accomplish things only to feel OK about myself, as if I needed to fix what was done to me. I realized that things were already OK. There was nothing wrong in my life. I had everything I needed and I could do or be anything I wanted. I felt truly free for first time in my life, and I felt I had been given the gift of limitless potential and possibility.

Chapter 6
Living with Awareness

I created a new story for myself. It was the biggest story I had ever created.

I would marry Cathy, not just because I loved her, but because I would also be able to save her. My mind told me that everyone around her—her sister, her father, and the rest of her family—had created a story about her that she was sick and fragile, that they had to worry about what would happen to her and how her condition would progress. Maybe this wasn't actually what they believed, but my own story about the situation insisted that they did. In other words, I was creating a story about the story they had created.

I didn't see Cathy in that way. She wasn't sick at all. She had no visible symptoms of any kind of illness. In fact she was physically vibrant and stronger than me in many ways. She had incredible energy, and she never sat down for a minute. She was always cleaning or doing things for her nephews or doing something productive. She was a buyer in the fashion industry, and she had so many responsibilities that many days, she worked into the late hours of the night. She was and still is physically beautiful.

If you have ever seen an average-looking guy who had a girlfriend who was way too good-looking for him, you might say, "How in the world did that guy get that girl?" That was me, the guy who landed the chick way out of his league.

The possibility that I consciously created was that we would have a great life together. I decided that I needed to take care of her by giving her a future based on optimism and the intention of happiness no matter what might occur. She in turn would give me the same thing. We got married in 1993 and had a huge wedding with our many friends and relatives. Between the two of us, we had so many close friends that our wedding party alone consisted of thirty people. Even my parents, who were both remarried for many years, and who still held on to their own stories about each other, decided that if their children were going to be getting married, they would become friends with everyone involved. We weren't going to play those kinds of division games that other families might play. To this day, I attend holiday dinners at my mother's or my father's house where both parents and their spouses will attend. In fact, people are surprised by what good friends those two couples have become, so much that they all call each other on the phone or actually go out for dinner together without any of the kids. We decided that we were an enlightened family—also another little story we created.

The first year we were married, several families we met at NIH, where we had been going for

Living with Awareness

Cathy's checkups, put themselves on television talk shows to raise awareness for VHL. One such family from Chicago appeared on an episode of *The Jerry Springer Show* at a time when Jerry still hosted serious topics, before he devoted his entire show to people arguing and cheating. (If you ever want to see people trapped in a mind-created story, watch a show like that.) Cathy and I watched our friends from Chicago on television, and were shocked when we saw the heading on the screen: "This entire family is dying." We couldn't believe that this is how they viewed their lives. The father had passed away due to the disease. He left behind his wife and four children. All four children, who now ranged from ages eighteen to twenty-eight, had varying VHL-related problems. The most severely affected sibling was the eldest brother. He had multiple tumors in his kidneys, and his doctors in Chicago decided to remove both of them. His situation was similar to that of many other VHL patients.

We noticed something else through our discussions with other patients. Depending on what doctors you had, where they practiced, and what they knew about this newly discovered condition, the treatment would vary. For example, at the NIH, doctors chose to watch one or many cysts or tumors until they reached a certain size, and then they might decide to take out the ones that they thought were posing a real threat. Some doctors, like the ones we heard about in Chicago, would remove an entire organ on the premise that, for instance, all kidney tumors would eventually lead to kidney cancer, so it is better to remove the organ before tumors ruined it anyway. The NIH had hundreds of families in their study data, and they were not so quick to make such drastic decisions. We learned early on that doctors didn't know everything, and it was up to us to turn the doctors' findings into a treatment decision. We made up a story that if the doctors in Chicago had seen Cathy's kidney scans, she might have lost her kidneys already and been on dialysis for the rest of her life. But her kidneys were fine after having a big tumor removed, and we were happy to just keep an eye on the smaller ones.

    The family on the television show was fighting with each other. They were in a panic. They had conflicting opinions about how they should all be treated, and which doctors to use. The most striking thing about them was the position they all took. They actually lived in a story that said they were all dying, and it was just a matter of time before VHL got them all. To a certain extent they were right. They would all eventually die, just like everyone else who had ever lived. The disease put all VHL patients in a vulnerable position, exposing their mortality. But to resign themselves to the story that they were all dying—it was against everything Cathy and I stood for. We had created a much better possibility for our future, and whether we were right or wrong about it didn't matter. They were trapped in a story, and we were living into a possibility.

Living with Awareness

• • •

Just three months after Cathy and I were married, FOX 5 learned about VHL. They were doing a medical story at the NIH, and they ran into Frankie. They learned about a family who had a little boy who lost his eye from VHL tumors, and they learned about Frankie and Cathy's family. The name of the show was called *Front Page*, and it was a nationally syndicated news show on the FOX 5 network.

They interviewed a number of families. When they met us, however, they seemed to shift the news story's emphasis. They saw that Cathy was such a pretty young woman who had just gotten married. Maybe it's just a story I created, but it seemed like we were the cute young couple that would appeal to the public, so the show became all about Cathy and me. All the other members of her family became "Cathy's cousin" or "Cathy's sister" on the subtitles. The story even showed clips from our recent wedding video. The show aired on Christmas Eve, 1993. Everyone we knew was calling us because they had seen the promotional commercial with Cathy saying, "When I found out I had this disease, I thought it was a death sentence." We thought it was a big deal, having them a do a whole television show about us. We thought it would raise awareness for VHL, so it would be a good thing. When it aired, we saw Cathy's doctors from the NIH; we watched ourselves answering questions; we saw the clips from our wedding; and we laughed about how some of our friends who made little video speeches at our wedding were broadcast nationally.

The station made it into a dramatic story. They didn't care about spreading awareness of the disease. They just wanted a human-interest story, and we fit their bill. We kind of felt exploited. The funny thing about seeing a television show about your life is that it reminds you how many different stories you can create from reality. At one point in the show, the narrator said, "Cathy and Greg had a beautiful wedding and they are very happy, even though they don't know how much time they will have together." My mind has never let me stop hearing that silly line from that silly show.

• • •

We used our gift money from our wedding to buy a house. Three months later Cathy was pregnant. Doctors told us that our child would have a 50 percent chance of inheriting VHL.

We had discussed it many times. We wanted our own child, and we came up with many reasons why we should have just one. We decided that Cathy's life was worth living. Whenever we heard people with VHL talk about never having children, we would remind ourselves that if Cathy's parents had thought that way, Cathy would never have been born. We didn't see Cathy's condition as something so unbearable that she would be better off not having lived at all. That just seemed silly. We also knew that Cathy's condition required treatment, but we decided that it was like going to the dentist, only sometimes a lot more uncomfortable, but we would bear it and then keep on going with our normal life like everybody else. After all we had seen with VHL, early treatment seemed to us like an actual cure. Pregnancy had special risks for Cathy. It wasn't that she had to watch for anything different from any other pregnant women, but she was unable to be scanned for tumors during her pregnancy. The NIH doctors watched her closely, but for nine months, whatever happened inside her body would have to go unobserved until she delivered the baby. It was a risk that we accepted. One day, late in Cathy's pregnancy, she went to the bathroom and produced a toilet full of blood. We were sure she had lost the baby. It was a scary moment for us, and as we were preparing to rush off to the hospital, I remember telling Cathy not to think. Thinking in moments like this always got in the way of taking the necessary actions. Thinking didn't matter. It never does. Thinking about something will never change anything, no matter how hard the thinking mind tries to be in control of the situation. Whatever was going to happen was already in progress.

We got to the hospital, and our pediatrician met us, did an ultrasound, looked at the screen, and said, "Here's your baby right here. Nothing is wrong. Sometimes pregnant woman have some bleeding. It happens all the time."

Our son Jesse was born in the summer of 1995.

• • •

We wanted Cathy to be able to stay home with the baby and not have to work. This was not as easy as it sounds. Living in North Jersey with a mortgage and two cars and child expenses was not cheap. Cathy's job as a buyer in the fashion industry paid well, but her late hours and the necessity of having to put our baby son in childcare was unappealing. I had a job as a salesman, but it didn't pay much; in fact, at that time Cathy was making a lot more than I was. I needed to create a story where I could keep my job, because in our situation, medical insurance was absolutely vital, as was somehow replacing Cathy's salary. So if I was not going to quit my current job so that we could keep the medical insurance, I had to find a way to make an extra fifty thousand dollars a year by just working on the weekends. That's a thousand dollars a week extra on the weekends. I knew I would need to create a pretty damn good plan to do that.

Awareness Means Choice

I racked my brains trying to come up with a solution to this difficult problem. A year earlier, our nephew had a birthday party, and we thought it would be cool to have a clown show at the party. I looked in the yellow pages to find a clown. When I called, the guy on the phone told me he charged $250 to show up for an hour. He said he would do a magic show, play some funny clown games, and make balloon sculptures for everyone at the party. I realized that it would be cheaper to actually buy a cheap clown suit, figure out how to make some balloon sculptures myself, go to a magic shop to buy a few tricks, and actually be the clown myself. So I did that, and I looked like a clown, and I twisted some balloons into shapes and I attempted to do some magic tricks and put on a show. It was not very good, but the kids liked it, and all the parents were laughing, so I was a good uncle.

Now, I considered the possibility of getting a really good clown suit, and learning how to make really great balloon sculptures, and learning how to do some really great magic tricks. I calculated that clown I talked to on the phone only had to do two shows on Saturday and two on Sunday at $250 a pop to make a thousand bucks a week, so that was my answer. I would be able to keep my job during the week, keep my medical insurance, and make a thousand a week doing clown shows on the weekend.

A lot of people I know would just try to get a better job, or they would take a second job on the weekend or at night, and that would have seemed like a very responsible thing to do, but it wouldn't have been enough. There wouldn't be enough hours in the week to make the kind of extra money I needed. Granted, I was not trained in any way to do this. I knew nothing about the business. I knew nothing about putting on a magic show or any kind of show at all. Doing this thing was all just a possibility I created because I had one conversation on the phone with one person who seemed to be making a living as a clown. The main thing—and really the only thing—that allowed it to happen was the saying of the words, "I'm going to break into the clown business." The saying of the words made it real. The saying of the words turned it into a plan. The saying of the words took the idea out of my mind and put it into the world.

I worked my crappy sales job all week, taking home about $500 every Friday. I stuck to my plan that would essentially allow me to triple my salary immediately. Cathy quit her job and was staying home with the baby. I started putting together my list of things I had to do to make my idea happen.

I always used lists to make my ideas happen. When I built the pizza place, I listed all the things I thought I needed to do to build the place. When I opened the employment agency, I did the same. I would put every little thing I could think of on my lists. The lists I would make would actually be the story I was writing about myself and how things would happen. The things I needed to buy would be on the lists as well as the things I needed to do.

The clown business was really pretty simple to figure out. My first list looked something like this:

1. Buy a clown suit, wig, and a rubber nose.
2. Take a class on applying clown makeup.
3. Learn how to make balloon sculptures.
4. Learn how to do magic tricks.

The trick to successfully starting up a new business is to try to think of every single little tiny thing that you need to do to make the business pen, and then do those things. As you go along a start crossing things off your list, you will realize new things to do that you never thought of. I have learned that as long as I kept crossing things off my lists, eventually the business would get started. I would not only include things I needed to do to start my business on these lists; I would put everything I needed to do in my everyday life, like pay the electric bill or pick up cereal and milk. The lists made me a productive person. I noticed that once I got through all the things I had to do on the list, I was in such a habit to adding to the list, that I would start looking for things to keep adding so that I would always have a list of things to do. By doing this, I was getting through all the things that I had to do, and all the things that I wanted to do, also. There has rarely been a day in my entire adult life that I did not have some sort of list in my pocket.

    Here's the key point, thought. This time around, I was also learning to notice the story in my head and decide if it was helping me or hindering me. My mind told me a few things about what I was doing. It told me that being a clown was not a cool thing to be. It told me that being a clown was actually kind of a weird thing to be. But I knew how not to listen to my mind. Actually it made me feel better that it was such an unusual thing to do to make money. I decided that it meant not many people would do it, therefore, my willingness to do it warranted me being paid a lot of money.

that I could decide what something
_ind always told me what something
ld decide if I wanted it to mean
_..d change the interpretation in my
_. ъy doing this, I couldn't actually change the
stories in my head about the past, but I could add
new possibilities about what those events might have
meant. I could spin negative experiences into positive ones. I could decide how times of conflict were
actually more valuable to me than the easy times. I
decided that the reason I knew how to create what I
was creating was because of all the things that have
happened to me so far. I had the power to decide
what anything means because I was realizing that
nothing really means anything.

I bought self-instruction videos on magic
and balloon sculptures. I visited magic shops often.
I practiced all the time. I filled up the living room
with balloon sculptures. Cathy had to throw out
garbage bags filled with twisted balloons. I performed my new tricks for everyone who would
indulge me. I brought tricks and balloons to every
family party so I could practice. I took a class in
applying clown makeup, and bought a professional suit. If anything, I would look the part, do a
few really great tricks, and twist a few really great
balloons.

I also needed to develop an act. I designed
a routine where I would introduce myself by saying
something funny and making something disappear
so that I could establish myself with the crowd. I had

some good things to do for the crowd, but I needed a lot of good things to say. I got books of one-liners from comedians like Henny Youngman and Steven Wright. I took all their best material. I decided that I would be like a cover band for jokes. I was ready to put on a show.

I was good at putting on a show. It was kind of like what I had been doing my whole life. I used to put on a show for the people at their doorstep when I sold newspapers. When we had the hot dog stands, I would line up six buns up my arm and flip them in one at a time. When we had the pizzeria I would flip pizza dough over my head and spin it around and catch it. I even learned how to juggle three pizzas at once, and the people would stand behind the glass and watch me at the worktable. I had a list of comical things to say when I was cold calling in the employment agency. Everything I ever did required me to capture an audience and get them to like me. I made up a story that said I was born to do this.

Now I needed to get work. I knew I had no experience, and I had no reputation, so I decided that I should be cheaper than my competitors. I would only charge $145 for a one-hour show that would include magic, jokes, and balloon sculptures. I had my little act ready to go. I got a dedicated phone line with a voicemail service; I printed business cards and I made flyers. Since I was a salesman during the day, I would visit places located in mini-mall and supermarket parking lots. I would place my flyers on windshields of cars in every parking lot

I came across. That became part of my daily routine, and I got phone calls from it. I managed to get some gigs right away. I wasn't very good at first, but it didn't matter. I looked good, I had a clean colorful costume, I had a structure to my performance, people would laugh at my stolen jokes, and I would fill the party with all kinds of balloon sculptures so it always looked like I had accomplished a lot during my short visit. I was getting paid my $145 fee, and most people were even giving me a twenty-dollar tip on top of that. It was also nice that most people would pay me in cash—instant money.

    I was getting a gig or two each weekend using my flyers, and every time I did a gig I would hand out my business cards. Many times each gig would lead to another one, but the process was slow, and I knew what I needed to make. To reach my goal, I needed several jobs every Saturday and every Sunday. I realized that to really make my story happen, I would have to commit myself to being available every single weekend without exception. I never planned anything other than being available on the weekends so that I could book shows months ahead of time when they would come in. My mind told me that would make me successful, too, because most people would never be willing to take away all the weekends in their life.

    After doing a few dozen shows, I felt confident enough to approach some entertainment agencies to offer my services. These agencies would book shows for you and take a piece of the fee. Generally they would charge anywhere from $250 to $300 and pay me $125 for showing up and doing the show. I wasn't able to hand out my own business cards at these kinds of gigs, and they wouldn't lead to future gigs to build my own business, but they would keep my schedule full. I did a lot of them. It only took me a few months before I was taking six gigs a week, three on Saturday and three on Sunday. They were almost all birthday parties for young kids. Others were corporate parties for employees and their families; I would set up, do my magic show, tell some jokes, twist balloons, get in and out in an hour, load up my car, and rush over to the next gig.

My stage name was Meatball the Magical Clown. My mind told me that was not a very cool name. My mind told me that the guy I used to be wouldn't want to be known as such a ridiculous thing. He never would have imagined he would be a clown in the first place. Being a magical clown for kid's birthday parties was not very impressive, and usually everything I did was someway intended to impress people. But I was aware of that now. I wasn't trying to impress people anymore. I was just trying to make money for my family. Having a name like Meatball would put me in a position to be made fun of. My mind told me that my friends would not think I was as slick and cool as I used to be. But I actually liked going against my mind and being in control of my own life.

After a few more months, I got sick of giving away half the fee to agencies that were booking most of my shows, so I put my own ads in the yellow pages. Paying money to make more money was a good choice. I wanted to make a thousand week and only do a few shows, so by advertising, I could actually buy more business. I put display ads in four different telephone books. It cost about $500 a month, but I was flooded with calls and I could book my own shows at a full fee, $245 an hour plus tips—if the customer really liked the show, sometimes I would get a $50 or $100 tip. The business was turning into a real cash cow, and my little show was getting better and better. After my advertising and other expenses, my new little business was making well over a thousand a week, every week.

    I kept my day job and did clown shows for a long time. I would call my customers after checking my voicemails all day long. I was working hard, but I saw enormous potential in what I was doing. I wasn't going to let this one get away from me. I created another story about how I would make even more money. Since I was able to learn my magic tricks so easily by watching how-to-do-magic videos, I decided to create my own. I was friendly with the guy who made the video for our wedding, and approached him with the idea. I thought it would be different to have a clown on a video teaching magic. I would have a lot of step-by-step graphics to make it simple and easy to understand. I would even tell jokes and put a laugh track on it to make it funny. We built a set in my garage. We had a colorful curtain behind a desk with a bunch of clown props all around. We set up lights and made it look like a little television studio. My videographer friend came over for a week and we produced our own magic video called *Magic Made Easy with Meatball the Magical Clown*.

To be honest, I didn't think it came out great. I was not the greatest magician. I didn't need to be great to do my shows. I did an adequate magic show, and I was very good at making balloons, and I had a nice way with the kids, so everybody liked me and paid on time, but I would not say I was a qualified, professional magician teaching people magic on a video. That didn't matter, though. The video's cover sleeve looked great: It was a picture of a colorful clown doing magic. That was enough to get it sold. I convinced a magic distributor to include our video in his catalogue, and magic shops throughout the country began carrying it. We made some money at first, but after the initial orders, none of the magic shops ever reordered it. We actually lost money on the total endeavor, but I was happy to keep throwing shit up against the wall to see what would stick. Again, as I thought, our video wasn't that good—but we had done something cool by producing it, and it led to something else.

• • •

Another possibility I created to get business was that I would appear once a week at a local restaurant. There was a big pizzeria called Bachagaloops that had a reputation for being a fun family place with a piano and setup for kids' private parties, which would feature do-it-yourself pizzas. Bachagaloops even had a commercial on cable TV. The commercial featured a local celebrity named Uncle Floyd Vivino. Uncle Floyd played the piano and sang the Bachagaloops jingle. I thought I could approach the owner, offer him a really cheap rate for me to come in, walk around to the tables, perform magic tricks, and make balloon sculptures. He said it would be OK.

    I appeared every Wednesday, and he paid me seventy-five bucks to show up for two hours as the clown. I also got tips, so I usually made over a hundred bucks for two hours, but it wasn't about making the hundred bucks. It was about getting more business, and it worked out really well. I gave out my cards to everyone I met, and every kid who met me wanted me to come to his or her birthday party, so the weekly gig yielded tons of business. I wound up staying with Bachagaloops for eight years.

• • •

    One Saturday afternoon, I did a show at a gig called Wayne Day. It was a yearly town event that brought in thousands of people. The event was held on a huge field behind the local high school. Hundreds of tents, food venders, and different forms of entertainment were set up for the patrons. I was starting to get some local fans because I appeared weekly at Bachagaloops, which was also in town. My tent was filled with kids who knew me from my weekly gig.

    After I did my magic show, a guy who was about to perform in a nearby tent walked up to me. It was Uncle Floyd, the guy from the Bachagaloops commercials. He knew who I was because he was friends with Carl, the owner, and Carl told him that I was filling up his place every week. Floyd had watched my magic show, and he told me it was great. Coming from him, that meant lot. After I was done with my gig, I watched him play the piano, sing some songs, and tell some jokes.

Now, he was *really* great. He was calm, seasoned, and flawless in everything he did. We got to talking that day and became friends. I saw him another time at Bachagaloops and explained the business I had set up. He liked my story, and he told me a little bit about his.

Floyd Vivino had been a performer since 1964. He was an outstanding piano player, and he had worked as a comedian and singer for over forty years. Floyd had appeared in movies such as *Good Morning, Vietnam,* among others. He was best known for his TV show called *The Uncle Floyd Show.* It had developed a huge following in the New York–New Jersey area, and after twenty-four years, it was the longest-running television show in New Jersey TV history. Floyd had earned lots of money in the entertainment business, but when I met him, his best days were already behind him. Those were his words, not mine. To me, it seemed like a story he had created, but I didn't get into that with him. He had lost his multi-million dollar home after his divorce and was paying alimony and child support for two ex-wives and children from both marriages. At that time he was living in the top half of a two-family house with his current girlfriend. He still made money, though, and lots of it, and he told me how he was doing it.

Floyd still filmed his television show, on which a camera crew would follow him around to different restaurants, bars, and local businesses. He would just talk to people and be funny and people loved it. His current shows were on every day, and his reruns also aired several times a day, too. I thought he made a fortune having that show, but he said he didn't. After paying the camera crews, editors, and producers, he said he did OK, but that was not how he made most of his money. He had created the kind of local fame for himself that people were ringing his phone off the hook to get him for personal appearances. He would do a lot of sixtieth or seventieth birthday parties for people who had been watching him for decades. He also did a lot of town appearances, such as the one we were attending. He did sometimes book bigger gigs in New York or Atlantic City, hosting special events. His primary income, though, was small parties. He would get $500 to show up and talk on the microphone for half an hour. He just had to show up with his silly little hat, squeeze out a couple of jokes, say hello to featured guests, and leave. It was quick and simple, and he did tons of those. It was not uncommon for him to show up to twenty or thirty events in a week.

To me, that was real money. He loved how excited I got about it. He liked me and he wanted to help me.

Our magic video.

Floyd Vivino

Meatball the Clown creates balloon hats to entertain kids at Wayne Day on Sunday. The event drew approximately 25,000 people, setting a record.

• • •

Many years earlier, I saw how Jimmy Botbyle had created a job for himself in which he convinced a carload of kids to walk around to houses and sell newspapers. I was able to recreate what he had done and get myself a contract that allowed me to get larger commissions. That formula—looking at someone else's story and recreating it for myself—worked again when I opened my own employment agency and gave myself my old boss's job. Likewise, I looked at what Floyd was doing.

I observed how he put himself in a position to regularly obtain high-paying gigs. I did not think I was as talented as Floyd, not even close. He played the piano masterfully, and he was the king of the one-liners. He had so many funny things to say in every situation that in all his TV shows, he rarely said the same thing twice. He had a seemingly unlimited well of funny material, and I did not. I didn't consider myself a real entertainer. I was only an entertainer because I said I was one, but really, I just did the same show over and over. When I did parties, I said the same words, did the same tricks, and made the same balloons every single time. My mind told me I couldn't possible do what Floyd was doing. He had talent and I didn't.

But I didn't listen to my mind, because it was telling me a negative story. Instead, I created a story about how I would recreate Floyd's story but in a way that would fit for me.

I already had the little television set built in the garage from when we made the video, and I had my little partnership with Brett the videographer, so I invented another story for growing the business. I would start my own television show, *The Meatball the Clown Show*. I bought a puppet at the magic shop that was just like Uncle Floyd's famous puppet, Oogie. The guy at the magic shop even told me that my puppet had been sitting in his showcase for over twenty years, and it was the exact same brand as Floyd's.

    I came up with some ideas for how the show would be run. I knew I was not an actor, so I would not attempt to act. I would make up short sketches that required me to read things, give instructions, and ask questions to guests. These are things I thought I could do, so I wrote the show around what I considered to be my own acting limitations. Every show had a "Trick of the Day," in which I would teach a trick like I did on my magic video. We would open up letters from fans during a "Meatball's Got Mail" section. Of course, all the letters were fake, written by me and designed to be funny. I would interview guests who were always relatives dressed up in a costume. I used my brother and my cousin for all kinds of different roles. Nobody ever got paid, but we had a lot of fun. I even brought my wife, Cathy, onto the show. She became Gumball the Clown, Meatball's wife on the show and in real life. She would help me with crazy cooking recipes, and she would always be the female for any sketch or fake commercial we would create. Cathy wasn't enthusiastic about dressing up as a clown and being on my silly show. Cathy was an Italian princess and she had much better things to do with her time, but she indulged me and put up with it.

I thought the show was funny, and a lot of people agreed with me. I gave a copy to Floyd, and he said it was very comfortable to watch. He liked the interaction of the characters, and he thought it would work. Floyd talked to the guys over at Comcast Television and persuaded them to air our show every Friday at 8 p.m. He even told the Comcast people that he was a friend of mine, and he would be appearing on the show frequently. We filmed ten separate segments with Uncle Floyd and me doing different things like goofing around his piano, or Floyd giving advice to Gumball and me about one topic or another. We wound up creating six full episodes, and we showed those six in rotation for two years.

We started to actually get real fan mail. People liked our show. The kids who came to see me in the restaurant watched it, too. My phones were ringing. So many people wanted to have the TV clown attend their kid's party. Other restaurants contacted me, too. They wanted me to appear weekly, just like at Bachagaloops, so I took on three more weekly appearances.

I was not even close to being the best clown or magician around. I knew many clowns and magicians who were much better than me. They were highly trained and had been doing it for decades, and they did pretty well for themselves. But I knew how to do something that they didn't. I knew how to keep creating stories to allow me get business. After just a few years, I was getting more business than any other local entertainer I knew because that was my area of expertise—getting business—and I realized that I could continue creating ways to get more and more. If something wasn't working, I could just take a different approach until it did work. There was nothing in the external world that could stop me, because as long as I didn't see the problems that would occur as a reason to stop, I would never have to stop succeeding.

• • •

In the meantime, I worked during the week as a salesman. It was an easy job. I would visit different pharmacies and talk to the pharmacists and the non-foods managers about putting the products I represented onto their shelves. I never saw a boss. I had the freedom to come and go as I pleased, and I could make my phone calls to customers whenever I needed to. Cathy stayed home with the baby, and she started to take calls from customers, too. Most evenings I would appear in restaurants, walking around doing magic and making balloons. On the weekends my schedule was usually full, meaning three or four shows in a row on both Saturday and Sunday. With the Yellow Pages advertising I was doing, and the TV show running every Friday, and giving out business cards in the restaurants, I was getting all the business I could do.

We started to give out work to other clowns and magicians. We developed a network of all kinds of private entertainers who were available to work. Cathy started booking all our shows. She would first make sure my schedule was as full as it could be, and then she would give out all the excess to the other entertainers. We would have customers send us a seventy-five-dollar deposit, which we would keep, and the entertainers who worked for us would keep the rest of the fee when he or she did the show. It was a pretty good system, and after a while, the piece of the fee we would get for sending out other people added up to more than my entire paycheck from my day job. Actually it started seeming kind of ridiculous to work all week for less money than I would make in just two hours on the weekend, but I kept the job for the company car and the insurance.

    Cathy started noticing how many people wanted female clowns, and after sending out dozens of them, she decided that she could just do the shows herself, so I trained her to do some magic and make balloon sculptures, and she started to do shows herself. This was a major turning point for our business. My doing six to eight shows a week myself at $245 plus tips was great, but having her start getting five or six shows herself at the same fees was something else. We could keep her entire fee, and the money was just rolling in. We made money from my shows, her shows, and the other entertainers. For a while we even hired a guy to send out moonwalks, popcorn and cotton candy machines, and carnival games. That worked out for a little while, but nothing was as sweet as just booking the shows. We decided to just specialize in that.

I was too busy to make any more TV shows, but it didn't matter. We just kept showing the same six episodes over and over. The TV show was really just an ongoing commercial for our services, but it didn't last forever. A few local businesses ran commercials during our show, which paid to keep it on the air, but we didn't make any money from it. We aired for two years until Comcast restructured their channels and stopped airing paid television. We didn't need it anymore, though. We were established. We had done so many shows and given out so many business cards that people just knew about us from seeing us somewhere. The more shows we did, the more shows we would get. We were growing exponentially.

During those years, the economy was thriving. There were millions of kids in North Jersey, and it seemed like all of them were having birthday parties for which parents would purchase some form of entertainment. The market was huge, and our little business was not so little anymore. Meatball Productions was averaging thirty to forty parties a week with Cathy and me doing most of them and farming out the rest. It was like people were throwing hundred dollar bills at us every single week.

Chapter 7
Find the Power to Create

As Jesse started getting older, Cathy decided to go back to college to get a degree in teaching. She needed to be busy, and she wanted to go back to work when Jesse went to school. She thought that teaching would give her the same, summers-off schedule as our son. Staying home and booking clown shows all day was not what she wanted to do with her life. With all the money we were making, we were able to put her through college, put Jesse in private school, and pay for anything else we wanted. Money was not a problem anymore. We could do and buy anything we wanted. She graduated and got a job as a special education teacher at a school just one mile away from our house. We continued to go to the NIH every six months for Cathy's check-ups.

We had medical issues to deal with during that period. Six months after Jesse was born, Cathy had to have a brain tumor removed from her cerebellum. It had grown at what we were guessing was an accelerated rate because of the hormonal implications of being pregnant. Again, this is one of the things we will never know for sure, but that is the story we created about it.

My mind told me to be very scared. The doctors seemed to have a pretty good plan for getting it out. We spent two weeks at the hospital in Bethesda. They took it out, she recovered, and a few weeks later, it was like it never happened. We continued on with our life. She also had small tumors in her eyes that needed treatment. We visited the top doctors in New York City, who would laser the microscopic tumors every few months. We always needed to visit doctors, and the network of physicians we had developed were some of the best in the country. We were lucky in that way. The surgeons at the NIH were the top people in the country, and the New York eye doctors had reputations for being the best ophthalmologists money could buy.

Certain things were free. Certain things were covered by insurance, and certain things cost money. The NIH was always free because Cathy was part of a study there, but the eye doctors in New York were not. They didn't even take insurance and they dealt with mostly rich people, but we never had any problems paying for whatever we needed. We got MRIs and CAT scans and ultrasounds whenever she needed them. My mind told me that I had problems that most people didn't have. My mind told me that I had to make more money than most people need because I would always have higher medical costs than most people ever have. I heard my mind as it would tell me that, but I used it as a justification

Find the Power to Create

for making lots of money. I told myself that I probably wouldn't be making so much if I didn't have to.

My mind also told me that I needed to be completely self-sufficient, and I couldn't work a regular job like most people because there would always be times when I needed to take days off to handle Cathy's medical needs. If we needed to go to the NIH for a few weeks, I would do it. Most companies only gave people a few weeks a year for vacation, total. My mind told me that we needed vacation time and medical needs time, and no company would ever be able to accommodate all those things, but I decided that I was in control of my life and I could create it to look any way I wanted it to look—and of course, I was right.

Cathy was working as a teacher now, and that opened up another door for me. My mind had the justification it needed to finally quit my day job. She was getting medical insurance for the family, and I could easily afford to give up my company car. Could I have quit sooner and focused on my business? Yes, of course. I was making enough money to buy private medical insurance, but my mind was such a responsible mind that it wouldn't let me do it. My mind grew so attached to the system I had created that it was very reluctant to allow me to change anything because everything was going so well. I was aware of what my mind was telling me, but I was not so enlightened as to be able to completely detach myself from its wants and needs. But I did quit my day job and become a completely self-employed person once again.

• • •

Not having my day job gave me freedom. I loved being able to take my son to school every day. I loved being there in the afternoon to pick him up. My only obligations were to call back customers when they left messages. The phone calls to customers did not involve a lot of back-and-forth negotiations. I had a good reputation, so most people who called had already made up their minds about hiring us. All I had to do was take a few phone calls every day to keep my schedule full. Almost every call resulted in my filling out one of our appointment cards with the show details.

I also had to show up at the restaurants for two hours in the evenings, and I would do all the shows on the weekends, too. Even if I did ten shows in a week, I would only have to work about twenty hours a week. My mind told me I had created the most amazing work situation possible. I used to take home thousands of dollars every week, and it was like I only had a part-time job.

Most shows took place on the weekends because that's when people threw parties. I noticed something else, too. People would spend a fortune on these parties. I attended so many first birthday parties where parents would rent out a fancy banquet hall, cater it with expensive food and drinks, and invite hundreds of people. First birthday parties started looking like weddings. Of course people had to hire an entertainer like me. It was expected. Rich people were trying to outdo each other. We were still in the middle of a boom in the party business, and it seemed like people just couldn't spend enough money. They hired DJs, motivational dancers, psychics, stilt walkers, inflatable moonwalks, carnival games and even big rides that made backyards look like theme parks. For people who did what I did, there really wasn't much competition to speak of because there was a limited amount of qualified clowns and magicians in the area.

My mind created a story that said I had achieved financial success, and I agreed. I could do as many shows as I wanted to, and I could make as much money as I desired. I developed a network of daycare centers and pre-schools that invited me to work at birthday parties. I started to get a lot of shows during weekdays—something new.

I ended up with yearly contracts for school functions, town picnics, churches, temples, and organizations. We did holiday parties, picnics, and all kinds of other parties for every police department and fire department in the area. We picked up all sorts of corporate accounts, too. Any and every organization had some sort of use for us at one or more times during the year, and the more shows we did, the more we would get—guests would later hire us for their own, smaller functions. It was an endless cycle. I had done thousands of shows, and as long as I remained able-bodied, our success would continue.

I had lots of free time on my hands. Sure, I always had to book shows and perform at certain times, but it became second nature to me. I didn't have to think about it as I was doing it. I would say the same things to customers as I was booking their parties, and when I was even doing my shows, I was on automatic pilot. After doing it so much, a show where I was telling jokes, doing magic and then making balloons sounded to me like, "Blah, blah, blah," twist, twist, twist... And *poof*, I was gone. They all started running in to each other. I was saying the same words and doing the same actions over and over and over again. I had mastered every single aspect of the business, so I didn't need to spend any extra energy thinking about it at all.

    I worked weekends, and most people I knew worked weekdays, so I needed to fill my time. For a while, I played golf in the afternoons. Another time, I enjoyed playing in Texas Hold 'Em poker tournaments in Atlantic City. I wasn't a gambler, but believe it or not, I was pretty good at it. I would win almost every time. If you have ever seen poker tournaments on television, I would be the kind of player that made it to the final table every time. I even started spending my free time playing in online poker tournaments. I got a kick out of it. One time I won a tournament on the Internet against twelve hundred other players. I could almost see why my father thought he could make a living playing poker so many years ago, but I wasn't about to try it. Poker was fun, but the easy money came from doing shows.

Find the Power to Create

My mind started to tell me that my business was sort of like a scam I was pulling on the world. I started questioning what I was doing, and how I was contributing to society. Other clowns and magicians told me the stories they created about themselves, which almost always said they were spreading happiness and making children laugh and all that other crap, but my mind wasn't buying it. I was good with kids and I did enjoy making people laugh, but I was in it for the money.

Also, I loved what I had created. I loved when people laughed at my jokes and applauded at the end of my show. I loved when people told me how great I was. My mind needed that. My mind needed constant approval. My mind loved the attention, because it needed to be fed with constant praise, and that is what drove me—I was aware of that. I was aware that my life was about feeding my mind's needs, and I wasn't sure that I liked that.

I saw other magicians and clowns who had been doing this for a lifetime. It seemed like they started to go a little nuts after a while. I knew this one clown named Peter who had been doing shows his entire life. He made up a lot of reasons to get angry with customers. He never wanted anyone to videotape his show because he thought people would steal his act. He hated when kids would interrupt him and throw off his timing. He hated when anything did not go according to plan. But things always happened at parties—people showed up late, and the entertainer would have to wait until all the guests arrived. It was part of the job, but Peter would charge them extra or threaten to leave. Peter was so crazy after so long that I even heard stories about his cursing out customers who made any other request that fell outside the parameters he set when he booked the show. One woman at a party once asked me if I knew Peter the clown, because he told her to fuck off when she ran out to his car to ask him if her son could take a picture with him.

    I knew many other burned-out entertainers, and I vowed never to be like them. We weren't famous. We were at the lowest level of fame you could possibly achieve. I was the clown on the local cable channel, the clown whom people had seen at their favorite pizzeria, and the clown whom someone had seen at little Johnny's christening. I performed for hundreds of thousands of people and I had my share of local fame. My mind told me that I was the king of the low-level performing wannabes. But I never changed my show. I never thought I had talent.

• • •

    I needed the kind of intellectual stimulation that clown shows could not provide. It bothered me that I never graduated college. I knew I was smart, and I knew that back then, my mind had told me to quit so I could start making money. But now I had some money, and I had most weekdays off. I was done paying for Cathy's tuition. She had graduated and was doing well as a teacher. My mind told me that my goals for the business had been met. I needed

Find the Power to Create

another goal, because my mind told me that without a worthwhile goal, I was just spinning my wheels.

I was so used to having something to strive for, that once I got there, it was emptier than I imagined it would be. Making money for its own sake was unfulfilling, so I enrolled myself into the college I had quit so many years earlier.

I had neither agenda nor aspirations. My mind told me that no job would ever pay what I was making, so I set a goal to simply learn as much as I could and graduate. After an interview with the admissions office at William Paterson College, they agreed to let me register with the provision that I met at least a 3.0 grade point average.

I had never studied a day in my life, and I really wasn't even sure how to go about it. I read a book called, *What Smart Students Know*. I took the strategies outlined in the book very seriously, and I learned to figure out what my professors were looking for. I liked to read, and I thought I had a talent for writing. I kept a journal when we had the pizza place, and people who read it thought it was good, so I became an English Writing major. I began with only 24 credits, earned when I had gone to college before—but my grade point average was only a 1.2. I joked to Cathy that I had really excelled when I had gone as a young person.

College for the second time was great. I had none of the earlier distractions. I didn't have a bunch of my frat brothers around convincing me to skip class and go drinking. I didn't have to think about making money or what I was going to do with my life. My mind told me I was there for all the right reasons, to learn. And I learned everything I could. I paid attention to every word that was said in class. I spoke up whenever I could, and I studied hard for every exam. I spent hours preparing my schoolwork. I got really great at writing clear, focused, organized essays, and got A's in every subject. I felt I was going somewhere again, even though I didn't know where. I kept booking and doing all the shows, and I kept appearing in restaurants. I was still able to take Jesse to school every day and pick him up, too, even though we were both students now.

Find the Power to Create

The Meatball the Clown Show

Five-year-old Jesse

• • •

In my second year of college, Jesse's school sent Cathy and me a note that he was having trouble reading the blackboard. Just a few days before, he had been talking about how cool it was that his friends started wearing glasses, and Cathy and I thought he might be faking his trouble because he wanted glasses, too. We were afraid, too, because we always knew what we might discover. We took him to the eye doctor to get his eyes checked right away.

Jesse proved to be slightly nearsighted. The eye doctor also checked with a special lens for eye tumors, or angioblastomas. She saw something. It was like getting hit in the head with a brick. Cathy immediately started crying, and I saw how much that surprised Jesse. I told her to stop right away. I didn't want Jesse to get scared.

Cathy and I had always talked about how she didn't know she had VHL until she was twenty-two years old. It was true that she might have been able to save a lot of her vision in her left eye had she known sooner, but it was also true—so said our story—that she had not had to worry about the condition for her entire childhood, teenage years, and college years. She was blessed with the gift of not knowing, and we thought it was a good thing. We wanted that for Jesse.

I was afraid of what stories Jesse might start creating in his little head about such a problem. After we left the eye doctor, Jesse kept asking why Mommy was crying, and I told him that the doctor saw a little dot in his eye and he might have to get it lasered out. I told him it was no big deal, and really he didn't need to think it was a big deal, either.

My mind told me it was a big deal though. It fixated on the tumor in Jesse's eye constantly. Something happened—we found out that Jesse had a tumor in his eye so he must also have VHL. I interpreted meaning—Jesse would need to have surgeries for a lifetime. Jesse would suffer and have to deal with the implications associated with VHL. I made a decision about myself—this was a huge problem. I could not stop thinking about the problem. I loved my son more than anything I could ever imagine. I had been so protective of him for his whole life. I would never let him out of my sight, and I would watch him like a hawk whenever we were out of the house. The thought that something was growing in his eye was devastating. The thought that there was nothing I could do about it hurt even more.

Of course we would arrange for treatments, but the problem was that the treatments were necessary in the first place. My mind was like a demon that kept screaming in my ear: "Jesse has a tumor in his eye! Jesse has a tumor in his eye!" My mind pictured Jesse's sweet little head and his sweet little eyes with this evil, insidious thing embedded in a place it had no business being. My mind told me this should not be happening. My mind kept me up night after night thinking these same thoughts over and over. My mind took me over completely, and for weeks, I cried whenever I was alone.

Chapter 8
The Mind-created Drama

I created a new identity for myself: I was a man whose wife and son had an incurable disease. An identity is just a story, but if I ever explained my situation to people, they always agreed that I had a huge problem, that my life itself was a problem. That agreement fueled the story.

Of course, it didn't seem like a story. It seemed very real. Ask anyone. The story told me other things, too: The future was bleak and dismal. Life was like a war zone where the enemy was shooting bullets at my wife and my son; except that we would never ever get out of the war zone and the bullets would keep hitting them, and we would never know where they would hit next. My story said I could never feel safe, and that I had to live in the war zone forever and ever.

I had to pull myself together. I had to do shows and be funny. I was in college, and I had to function in the life I had created for myself. I had to be strong for Jesse and Cathy, and I had to make their lives all that they could be. I was taking a history course at the time, and the professor was trying to explain what it was like for ordinary people back in the 1700s. He showed all kinds of statistics about how short life spans were. He showed how limited medicine was back then and how the slightest illness could have resulted in death. He showed that if you had been fortunate enough to live to the ripe old age of sixty, you would have most likely witnessed the deaths of your spouse, all your friends, and some of your children. His lecture gave me some perspective. I felt fortunate to live in an era of advanced medicine. I grew more hopeful that I would be able to walk through my struggles.

    I watched doctors put my seven-year-old son under anesthesia, and I watched him wake up again without a tumor in his eye. I told him that the dot in his eye was gone, and if another dot grew somewhere else, we would get rid of that one, too.

• • •

    I learned everything I could in college. I was that annoying older student in the class who was interested in everything the teacher had to say. I read all the chapters in my textbooks and every required novel from cover to cover. As an English major, I found that I was able to learn about history and human nature in novels. I was like a sponge sucking up every bit of information I could get my hands on. I realized that with intense focus on every lecture, I could memorize almost every single thing every professor had to say on every subject. I realized that the story I had created from Mrs. Kostyra's action so many years ago was true. I was smart. I took thirty-two courses in order to graduate

The Mind-created Drama

from college, and I got an A in every single one of them.

I wanted to get a degree in something that I could actually use, so I decided to get my teaching certificate. I even had to be a thirty-nine-year-old student teacher for fifth graders. Because of my experience with clown shows, I was good with the kids. I watched and learned how to teach. I learned how to develop my own lessons. I did magic tricks and made balloon sculptures for the kids in my class, and at the end of the year, I put on a show for the whole school. I graduated with a degree in English Writing, a certificate to teach elementary school, and a certificate to teach English in middle school and high school. I was compelled to once again to create a new story for myself.

• • •

Teaching did not pay a lot of money. I was currently earning a six-figure salary thanks to the clown shows. Even in college, I did as many shows as I could, and after beginning to teach, I still appeared in restaurants. I also got into the practice of talking my restaurant customers into hiring an additional clown to do face painting while I performed my show. This worked out well for us because a lot of times we would get double the normal fee, and Cathy would come along with me and paint faces.

I found that I was constantly changing my clothes. I would wear a shirt and tie to teach, then I would have put a clown suit on to do my shows, then I would come home and put on sweats and sneakers. Cathy got annoyed because I produced more laundry in a day than anyone else in the world. Soon, however, I found it became easier to just bill myself as a magician. It was much easier than applying clown makeup every time I had to appear somewhere, and all it required was a tuxedo shirt, a bow tie, and my magic pants with suspenders. I became Mr. Meatball the Magician, and nobody seemed to notice the difference. I was never the clown again, and people seemed to respect me more when I looked like a normal person.

My mind told me that I was now an educated person. I knew that I had been chasing after money for my entire life. My life had revolved around the pursuit of money, and it started to seem silly. I wanted to teach. I wanted to make a difference in the lives of others. I wanted to do something with my

The Mind-created Drama

life that wasn't motivated by money. I liked the idea of being off in the summer, and ending my workday at 3 p.m. Teachers got many vacation days, and if I needed time off to address my family's medical needs, I could.

I had saved up a bunch of money in the bank, and I could now afford to be a teacher. I also could still do the weekend shows, so I had enough justification to make the change. Confident that I could earn what I needed to support us, I chose to make the business smaller. I gave up three of the restaurant gigs and kept the one where I made the most and saw the most people. It hurt—my mind didn't want to do it, but I was determined to use my life for a nobler cause. I took a job as a high school English teacher.

• • •

It was difficult to adapt to working for a school district. I had either been my own boss for most of my life or operated independently. And besides, I had a very different background from most new teachers. Most new teachers are young, right out of college. I came with a lot of stories built up inside me. The stories in my mind were so vast and full that I was like a computer with that was using up too much of its hard drive. Such a computer contained many files to draw from, but it might operate slower than a new computer because it had too many alternative choices for any single operation.

Having a lot of stories built up is like knowing everything about everything. Somehow everything that occurs in your life seems like something else that already occurred, and every time you meet someone, you apply your preconceived notions about who that person is. If someone looks like someone else that was a jerk, then you create a story about the jerk-look-alike even though you have no idea who that person is. Knowing a lot can come in handy when you need to apply certain skills to achieve a certain goal, but it can get in the way when you are looking for a fresh perspective.

I learned that I had to take responsibility for how I was perceived by other people. My mind would immediately create stories about every single person I encountered. It would never stop. Any time anyone said anything about anything, my mind instantly heard what they said, interpreted meaning, and made a judgment about what kind of person they were, producing a story about who that person was and what he or she was all about. I noticed that I was not the only one making up stories this way. Everyone did it all the time.

• • •

I had a difficult time my first year as a teacher. I took a job forty-five miles away from my house, and I needed to be in by 6:15 because classes for students started at 7 a.m. That meant I had to get up at 4:30 every morning. I had to be out by 4 p.m. on Wednesdays so I could get home early enough to change into my costume and get to the one restaurant gig I kept by 6 p.m. I used the time in the car

The Mind-created Drama

to call all the customers back and coordinate shows, which kept coming in like crazy.

When I was offered this first teaching job, I was actually in an interview for a position teaching the fifth grade. I had student-taught fifth grade already, and I thought I might start out small and work my way up. I was going to teach all the subjects, just as I had learned to do. The school district's English supervisor was present at the interview, however, because she had to fill a high school position immediately. She knew I had no experience, but she knew that I was an English major, that I was older than most of her applicants, and that I was a professional magician, so she thought I could handle the jump into the unknown. So did I, because my mind told me I could do anything, even though I barely even remembered going to high school.

Now when you're a teacher, there are some gigs that are generally considered harder than others. A good high school teacher situation might involve teaching one grade level and one subject. For example, you could teach only tenth grade English. You would have to prepare lessons for one type of course at one level of difficulty. It was harder, therefore, to teach more than one subject at more than one level of difficulty. Some teachers where I worked complained that they had to teach math for ninth graders and eleventh graders, meaning they had to do two "preps" per day.

I had four preps. I taught ninth, eleventh, and twelfth grade English, and one of my eleventh grade courses was an honors course so it had to be different from the eleventh grade regular course. That meant I had to prepare four different kinds of lessons every day, and any teacher will tell you that it is tough to do, especially when you have never taught English or in a high school a day in your life.

Generally, a high school teacher teaches all classes in the same room. This way, all your stuff like worksheets and lesson plans don't have to be moved throughout the day. Teachers get annoyed if they have to teach in more than one room. To make my gig even more difficult, I was to teach in five different classrooms located far away from each other. I would always forget something.

Also, teaching four different kinds of classes required me to teach a different novel for each class for all four of the marking periods. I never did any of the required reading when I was in high school, so now I had to read sixteen novels for the first time and prepare lessons for them.

My mind told me that I had a very hard schedule, and every teacher who saw my difficult schedule agreed with my story, and their agreement made it true. Whenever I tell this story to teachers I currently work with, they always say that this situation would have made the success of any new teacher absolutely impossible.

• • •

Cathy's eye doctor was starting to notice that a certain tumor in her eye was not responding well to laser treatments. The treatments were causing the

The Mind-created Drama

tumor to bleed, and they were afraid to keep treating it with lasers. They started trying a drug called Evasten that was injected into the eye directly to reduce the tumor size.

This was the first time that anyone had ever told us that they weren't sure if something would work. We knew of VHL patients who let tumors in their eyes get too big and lost their eyes. It was a scary situation for us. Cathy and I had to drive into New York City every two weeks to monitor her treatment. I would have to rush home from work, which was an hour's drive, then rush into city, which would take another hour, find parking, sit and worry in the waiting room, and go into the room and listen to great medical minds anguish over how they were going to save her eye, every single time knowing that they could say at any moment that they couldn't.

Also that year, Cathy had to go to the NIH in Maryland for her checkup and scans. My sister-in-law took her, and I stayed home with Jesse. Doctors found another large tumor growing in her brain. They told us that it would have to come out soon.

We lived with worry in our heads the whole year, on top of worrying about what might crop up in Jesse, on top of worrying about all the other things other teachers worry about all the time. My mind told me this was impossible. My mind told me I was choosing to be a teacher when I could just be choosing to do shows. My mind told me to be mad because I was not allowed to do what normal people did, like just work a normal job. My mind told me it was so unfair that I had to pay these New York doctors so much money for every visit. They didn't take insurance, and even if they did, she was on an experimental drug and insurance wouldn't cover it. The visits would cost a thousand dollars every two weeks and the drug alone cost thousands to buy every time they administered it. All my extra money was going to these doctors, and if I didn't make a thousand dollars every weekend, we would have been screwed.

I was lucky that I had the money, and no matter what anything cost, I could pay, but my mind told me I should be mad about it all the time. It told me that no one else would be able to do this, and it told me to be mad at anyone who would dare say they had it rough. My mind even brought back my anger toward my parents, who were doing so well these days. My mind told me it wouldn't be the worst thing in the world for my rich mother to give me some fucking money every once in a while to relieve my burdens. My mind repeated these thoughts for me over and over every day.

All these things were my problems, nobody else's. But I didn't see that at the time. I got mad if someone dared to criticize me in any way.

• • •

That year, I had what I feel quite comfortable calling the Supervisor from Hell. She liked me at first, and then she realized I had no idea how to teach English. I didn't. I never said that I did. It was agreed that I would learn as I went along. I was an English major in college, so I knew basic grammar, and I knew how to write effective essays, but teaching those things is an acquired skill. I actually thought someone would show me what to do, but nobody ever did. So I fumbled through it myself and made a lot of mistakes.

When the Supervisor from Hell realized I had no idea what I was doing, she immediately created a story about me that I was an idiot. At least that was the story that I created about the story that she created. She talked to me like I was a fool, and would stump me with her questions all the time. She was looking for ways to prove to me that I didn't know how to teach, and she always found them. It wasn't too hard. Some of the other teachers helped me prepare my four lesson plans a day, and I started to get the hang of it after a while, but I was doomed from the start.

The high school students smelled the newness on me. They knew I didn't know what I was doing. I would read novels with them and make comments as we read. I would go over vocabulary words and draw pictures on the board to visually represent each word. I showed them what I knew about writing essays: how to write an opening paragraph, a clear thesis statement, body paragraphs that supported the thesis statement, and closing paragraphs that wrapped up all the essay's main ideas. I was actually pretty good at teaching that part because I was really a writing major in college. I did my best to keep up with the curriculum, and I got along with the kids. I wasn't strict, and I was funny, and I was an easy A for anyone who did not give me trouble.

Yet my supervisor seemed to have her own notions about how an English teacher should look and act. And I didn't seem to meet any of her requirements. She would stand outside my door while I was teaching, and later, tell me that she cringed when she heard me trying to teach. She told me I always seemed nervous when she would come and watch my lessons. She was right again. She was looking at me so critically that I was never the same person as I was when she wasn't there. It was demoralizing. Conversely, the principal, a former gym teacher who observed me several times, always gave me praise for being prepared and enthusiastic. But his opinions did not affect my supervisor's.

I don't think anyone actually tries to be an asshole. I think they always have their reasons for treating someone poorly. Sharon, my supervisor, had obviously made up a story about me based on what she saw, our conversations, and our interactions. Now, no matter what I believe Sharon's stories said about me, they will only ever be my own stories, my guesses—but here they are. This woman viewed me as weak teacher. I knew certain teachers that she seemed to respect. They were teachers who were stern and strict. They were teachers who took themselves very seriously and acted deliberately in their classroom. I was funny and made jokes out of the material we covered. I thought I was allowing the kids to create lasting connections by doing so, but she just cringed and thought I was unprofessional. I created a story that said she always compared me to

The Mind-created Drama

all the others teachers in the department, who were all female, and she wanted me to teach like they did; that was the only way she knew English teachers were supposed to be, and I couldn't do it. I made up a story that I must have reminded her of her ex-husband who had left her and her kids many years ago. I made up a story that she hated all men. I was struggling with my schedule, working weekends, and dealing with serious medical issues, but this woman saw a man who was probably letting his problems at home affect his work performance.

I don't think she ever considered that I probably looked unorganized all the time because I had been given the most impossible workload in the school, and I was a first-year teacher. I don't think this woman ever trained a brand new teacher before, because most of the problems she criticized me for were always related to being new.

There was nothing good I could do in Sharon's eyes, and it was evident. My mind told me that her assertions about my teaching abilities were overblown. Because I was a first-year teacher, my mind concluded that I couldn't have been expected to know what a seasoned teacher knows, so therefore she is declaring that not only am I not good now, but also that I lacked the qualities to ever become good in the future. Why else would someone be pushed toward termination in his first year?

My mind was offended. It said, "Doesn't this person know who I am and what I've been through? Doesn't this person know how successful I am and how much I am capable of?" I hated her for not being able to see me for who I really was. But she couldn't, just as we cannot see most people for who they really are. We are so stuck in our mind-created stories and preconceived notions about other people that we rarely see past our own limited perspective.

By January of my first year, and after receiving three poor written evaluations in a row, I knew that there was no way I would be rehired for the following year. I knew I wasn't weak. I was not like other teachers she knew. My work situation was not the big deal she thought it was, and her power as a supervisor was all just a story, too. Similarly, I had worked hard in college and I knew that going through my first year as a teacher was supposed to put me on a track towards tenure, so my mind created a story that this job was more important than it really was.

My work situation was really just a game that I was playing, nothing more. I needed to treat it like a game because that would take the seriousness out of it. I didn't need the money that the job provided. I could replace my teaching salary by just taking a few daytime shows during the week. I looked at the situation carefully. I knew it was an hour's drive from my house, and I didn't want to always wake up at 4:30 in the morning. I knew I never wanted to have to deal with this witch of a supervisor ever again. So I scheduled a meeting with her, and this is basically what I told her: "According to you, I am not a good teacher. My lesson plans are less than they should be, and my

The Mind-created Drama

teaching style is undesirable. I believe you. I believe everything you are saying, and as a believer of what you are saying, I cannot in good conscience carry on here as a teacher. It is not because I am new, and it is not because I have four different preps in five different classrooms—it is because I don't listen to your guidance and I don't possess the necessary traits to do this job. I definitely don't have enough experience to be who you want me to be, but you did know that when you hired me, so maybe you shouldn't have done that. Therefore, I will leave whenever you think I should, and know that I will not be seeking employment here in September. Actually, if I am as bad as you say, I probably should leave as soon as possible."

Anyone who listens to you automatically creates stories based on what you say, so if you are careful about your words, you can control what kind of stories they create. I intended for her to create the following story: *This guy does have what any teacher or administrator would consider an impossible schedule, and he is new, and I did hire him, so maybe I am responsible for his failure here. He can't leave in the middle of the year because that would make me look like I didn't give him the support he needed. If anyone ever hears the reasons he just gave me for why he should leave, I will look bad.*

I don't know for certain what stories she created from our conversation, but I do know that she left me alone for the rest of the year after that, and I was free to pursue another teaching job. I found it after just one interview; I was pretty good at this part of the process, because my job for five years in the employment business was to tell people what to say and how to act on interviews. I spent the rest of the year figuring out how to teach, and I was able to do it without the pestering of my annoying supervisor.

• • •

The New York eyes doctors had Cathy undergo another experimental procedure to reduce the size of her eye tumor. It was called photodynamic therapy (PDT). They injected a chemical into her bloodstream, and then they put her into a dark room and blasted the affected areas in her eye with light. The drug was designed to cut off the blood flow to cancerous growths in the body. The drug would only react when it was exposed directly to light, and the light was carefully directed into the right areas during the procedure. She did, however, have to leave the office wearing long sleeves, gloves, sunglasses, and a big hat, because if any other areas of her body were exposed to sunlight, the drug in the bloodstream would burn the exposed areas. She was like a vampire. We had to keep the windows drawn for most of the week after the procedure.

It worked, though. The blood flow to her tumor was cut off, and it shrank down to a size that it could be effectively lasered without bleeding. We felt like we had dodged a bullet.

• • •

The summer after my first year as a teacher, Cathy had brain surgery at the NIH. We left Jesse

The Mind-created Drama

with Cathy's aunt. She checked into the hospital, and they gave me a room at the Safrah Family Lodge across the street.

This was the second time Cathy needed brain surgery. Just the words, "brain surgery," bring all kinds of stories along with them. We saw the possibility of unfavorable outcomes all around the hospital, and we were always scared, but we knew by now not to discuss our fears. It didn't matter if we were scared. She still had to undergo the surgery, so being scared and embellishing that story wouldn't change anything. It was much better to be positive and determined to kick the tumor's ass.

The doctors explained how this tumor was much bigger than the one she had removed years before. They expressed their fear of waiting any longer to extract it because it was too near the brain stem, and it was producing cysts that could drain out and cause something called hydrocephalus, and that could kill you instantly. We happily agreed to get that bastard tumor out of her head.

I waited in the room across the street during the surgery. My mind was producing fearful thoughts. It never let me see things optimistically when high-risk things were happening. My mind threw a barrage of negative, scary thoughts into my head, so I made myself fall asleep for as long as I could to escape my mind's unbearable drama.

Hours later, I got the news: Everything had gone well, and Cathy was recovering in the ICU.

• • •

I was always amazed at how weak and fragile Cathy was after a surgery, and how quickly she returned to health afterward. This brain surgery had left her in the weakest condition I had ever seen. I watched the nurses change all the tubes that were inserted in various parts of Cathy, clean her incision, change her IVs, and move her into different positions. She seemed as frail as a sick bird, but she managed to say hi and give me a smile. I could tell that we—really she—had gotten through another one of these damn things.

After a day, Cathy was moved out of the ICU and into a regular room. Another day and she was able to sit up, and a few days later, she was walking slowly around the hallways with her IV fluids rolling along next to her. A week later we were on our way home. She took it easy for a few weeks. The shaved patch of hair grew back, and soon our life carried on as though the whole thing had never happened.

• • •

The next fall I started my new job as a teacher, but before I get into that, I want to point out an interesting statistic reported by the U.S. Department of Education the year I left my first teaching job. It was titled "Fifty Percent of New Teachers Leave in 5 Years," and it said,

> The U.S. Department of Education reports that over the next decade, more than two million new teachers will walk into a classroom for their first day. Unfortunately, as the National

The Mind-created Drama

Center for Education Statistics found, 666,000 of those new teachers will leave sometime during the first three years of teaching and one million of them will not make it past five years.

I had a tough experience in my first year of teaching because being an effective teacher is much harder than most people think. You might say that I worked a year under extraordinary circumstances, but as the news story shows, half of all teachers make a decision to get out of the profession. I could have easily been one of them, had I decided that every teaching job I would take would be as difficult as my first.

Once people decide how something is, that's it. They think they know how it is. Every single situation is different—different people, different places, and a different set of circumstances. But people don't see that, and I often wonder how many of those new teachers ran into a difficult time because they were new and felt that teaching wasn't for them, after all. Apparently a lot, according to the statistic.

Something happens—teachers struggle through their first years. Meaning is interpreted—teaching is too hard. The decision is made—this is not for me. Say that is what happened to fifty percent of the new teachers who left. Such a decision is a big deal. Teachers go to college for four years, participate in student teaching, take the praxis test, interview, and teach demo lessons. It is not an easy job to get, yet after so many people get there, they up a story about why they should leave the profession, just as I used to do after I would build my businesses. When I had the hot dog stands, the pizza place, and the employment agency, I always had a good story about how to get there, but I didn't have a good story about how to stay there. It may seem like the external circumstances in any situation are what determine someone's success, but that is never the whole story. Once that person's story becomes, "I'm done with this," then it's over.

My new job was at a middle school ten minutes from my house. The students came in at 8 a.m., so I didn't have to wake up at 4:30 anymore. I was teaching only seventh grade classes, and most of them were at the same difficulty level except for one honors class. The seventh graders were much easier to deal with than high school kids; they were less arrogant, more like little kids on the inside who were just starting to look older on the outside. It was a much easier gig.

At the middle school, I was able to apply all the techniques I had learned at the high school. I was under such scrutiny my first year that, to fight off those who would criticize me, I learned how to create lesson plans that contained all the best elements of contemporary teaching practices. Only having one class-type a day freed me to create detailed lessons with all sorts of well-thought-out activities that allowed my students to make lasting connections to the material. Moving lower in grade levels made things easier; there was nothing unfamiliar in the

The Mind-created Drama

curriculum. Having student taught in the fifth grade as well as several grade levels in high school, I knew almost exactly where the students had been and exactly where they would be going. I was a much more qualified English teacher. I was still new, but I vowed to keep pretending to be a teacher. I knew that if I pretended to be something for long enough, eventually I would become it.

The game you play when you are a new teacher is the game of getting tenure, and whatever your preconceptions are about teachers, tenure is difficult. It takes three years. Having tenure only means that a teacher can't get fired without good cause, so the administration would have to build a strong case against you if they ever wanted to replace you. But tenure was what all the new teachers wanted, and there were fourteen of us who were brand new to this school district. All of us created the story that the most important thing was to get tenure. That story took on its own life, as if getting tenure would give us a permanent home in the school and we would live as teachers happily ever after. It sounds silly, but chasing after tenure can be a very important and frustrating thing for new teachers. I have known teachers who worked for three years, didn't get tenure, and had to start the process over again in another school, worked for another three years, not get tenure again, and start all over again elsewhere. A teacher can wind up working half their career as non-tenured if they are unlucky. Schools want to make sure they are getting the best person they can before they commit to them for the length of a career.

Since the tenure process is rigorous in New Jersey, and no administrator wants to be responsible for letting an unqualified teacher in, teachers are put under a microscope. To be able to continue on to the next year as a teacher in a school, you have to survive the observations. Maybe there are people who are perfectly comfortable speaking in front of a class and delivering a lesson while there is an adult in a suit sitting in the back of room, taking thorough notes, deciding the fate of your career. Even with my experience in performance, I never was able to be that person.

A teacher teaches an average of nine hundred lessons a year. A non-tenured teacher will be observed three times in a year. That is less than one-third of one percent of the time. You can be the greatest teacher in the world ninety percent of the time, but if you happen to get unlucky enough to be observed with a class that has one kid who decides to throw off your timing, or just be in between two great lessons with an average one, or just be having a really bad day and the lesson you designed isn't working, well, you stink. You stink because the observer saw you stink, and often all it takes is one time for that observer to see you stink and create a story about you.

In my first year, I was lucky enough to have been seen doing something good every time my observers visited, so I made it through to the next year.

The Mind-created Drama

I excelled in the middle school. The administration liked me and my peers respected me. My circumstances were better, and I became the teacher that I wanted to be. I was able to do things other teachers couldn't. I was a professional magician, and I made things disappear in the classroom all the time.

In my second year, they gave me a laptop computer, speakers, and a projector, and I figured out how to use them in ways nobody ever thought of. I piloted a program where I documented my efforts to use video clips, sound effects, music, and projections on the screen using various software programs. I figured out a way to use my laptop to project everything I needed to teach every lesson onto the screen in front of the room. I developed a system in which every time the lesson warranted a relevant movie, TV, or commercial clip, I would click an icon and that video clip instantly appeared at the right moment. For example, I could show the obvious high point of any movie to teach the concept of a story climax, or I could show an infomercial that followed the formula I use for teaching how to write an effective persuasive essay. A lot of times, I would just insert funny movie or television clips into the lesson just for laughs.

I realized that by being funny for no reason, students would create a story for themselves that my class was a lot of fun, and that made them all look forward to coming every day because they never knew what funny thing would happen next.

I also developed a series of audio clips that I would just click on to produce sound effects at certain times during the class. If somebody said something funny, a laugh track would go on to speakers I had set up around the room. If somebody gave a poor response, a crying baby would be heard. After a student presentation was made, I had various versions of stadium applause. It was like my classroom was a live situation comedy. And if students had to walk up to the front of the room to contribute something, I played a theme song for each student as they approached.

The variety of sounds coming from my room got every other teacher curious, and soon I was giving workshops to teach my techniques to teachers throughout the district. I was finally interested in something that had nothing to do with making money. My mind created a story that this was my calling. I was deliberate about my instruction, and everything I did was designed to allow the students to make connections that they would remember.

I knew all too well the stories children can create about themselves based on the actions of their teachers. Whether they realize it or not, students are affected by us in ways that always stay with them. I took and still take full responsibility for the power I possess as a teacher. I always tell the kids how great they are, and no matter who the student is, I always tell them how smart they are because maybe they might believe me.

The Mind-created Drama

After my third year in the middle school, only four out of the fourteen new teachers that I started with remained. All four of us got tenure, so we all created a story that said we are good teachers.

• • •

We dealt with a few medical issues during those years. Jesse got follow-ups for his eyes, which resulted in a few minor laser surgeries, but otherwise he was doing fine. We asked the NIH doctors about when we should start having him checked for other tumors, and they told us that even if they found some things, they usually didn't like to operate until the patient is fully grown. They simply told us that if he ever exhibited symptoms, we should call them immediately.

We were checking his eyes regularly, but we knew that within the next year or so, when he turned fifteen or sixteen, he would start having full scans. We weren't looking forward to having that conversation with him, but we knew eventually it would come. That thought stayed with me always, and I dreaded it. As Cathy had experienced, we wanted his youth to be uninhibited with worries about VHL. So far, Cathy had been the youngest patient in her family to start getting checked—she had been twenty-two. Jesse looked and seemed perfect even to his regular pediatrician, who was always on alert for anything unusual.

Cathy had several procedures over those years. Scar tissue had built up in her left eye where extensive laser surgery had been done over the years. The extra scar tissue was causing her retina to detach, and the doctors explained that the only thing preventing complete detachment was the tiniest thread of normal tissue. To prevent vision loss, she had to get a special surgery where doctors would laser the excess scar tissue between the two layers of her retina so that when it healed, it could attach to a clean area.

The surgery required an unusual healing process. Doctors explained that after the surgery, they would be somehow inserting a special gas to create a kind of air bubble underneath the entire retina. This gas would force the eye to stay in place by pushing upward on it, toward where the scar tissue had been removed. And in order for the gas bubble to push her eye straight back where the detachment was occurring, she needed to stay face-down for two weeks. At first we didn't completely understand what that meant, but then it was clearly explained that this face-down position was required for twenty-four hours a day, every day for a minimum of two weeks.

I don't need to explain the kinds of stories we created about such a daily inconvenience, but we were happy that the procedure would fix the problem. Our story has always been, "As long as there is a way to handle something, we are grateful."

I waited for many hours again, the way I have done a million times before, in the waiting room while the five-hour procedure was started and finished. Believe it or not, this was an outpatient procedure. I drove her home, nervous about every bump

The Mind-created Drama

or sharp turn on the way to the tunnel, and the traffic was horrible. Cathy was getting carsick, and I didn't know what her eye looked like under her bandages. She seemed so uncomfortable. My mind got me so upset about the whole situation that I even missed a turn toward the tunnel, adding another half hour of traffic to the trip, which in turn got me even more upset.

When we finally got home, Cathy lay down using one of those horseshoe-shaped pillows around her face. She passed the entire night like that, so uncomfortable that she didn't get a wink of sleep. The next day we had a special chair and a special bed device delivered from the medical supply store. These were designed to support the rest of her body while her head was face-down. The chair looked like one of those sitting massage chairs we used to see at the malls, but it was much more elaborate. The bed device was similar. We needed people to stay with Cathy during the days while I was at work. Cathy's sister and her aunt took turns living at our house, and they did all the cooking, cleaning, and everything else for us.

Even so, after just a few days of being face-down, Cathy started going out of her mind. This was not a good position, literally or figuratively. Cathy was the busiest person I knew, and not being able to do anything for herself was driving her nuts. It seemed like she took it all out on me, because she was yelling at me constantly and I knew I couldn't say a thing about it. I had to take a lot of abuse those weeks, but I understood. Cathy and I had been married for a long time already, and believe me, we fought about the same things most couples fought about—paying the bills, the floor on my side of the bed being a mess—and just because we were in the middle of medical crisis did not mean we didn't bicker constantly about regular stuff, too. We had an advantage, though, over most couples. We knew what was really important. Perspective was always there to punch us in the face.

    We got her a tilted mirror that allowed her to watch TV, and she suffered through it. It actually became comical, and we laughed about this absurd predicament. It was even more comical when we went back to the eye doctor's office after two weeks and he told her she needed to keep healing like this for another week.

    Cathy was eventually able to sit upright again. We continued visiting the New York eye doctors every two weeks for a long time, and eventually the time in between visits grew to every month and then every three months and then every six months. The surgery was a complete success, and we were so happy for the reprieve. As before, our minds gave us permission to immediately stop worrying about that one body part and enjoy our new lease on life.

• • •

    The next year, scans showed that Cathy needed another kidney tumor removed. This would be her third kidney surgery. Five years earlier she had an easy one, a radio frequency ablation (RFA). They were

The Mind-created Drama

able to just insert a probe that found where the tumor was on the kidney. They used the CAT scan machine as the operation was happening, and they were able to watch the image on the machine and monitor the probe's progress. When the probe reached the tumor, radio waves disintegrated it. Her kidney remained whole, and the only thing she was left with was a tiny hole in her back that healed up in a few days.

But now she needed a regular surgery with a knife because this tumor was too big for RFA. During our spring break, we went to the NIH together, and I graded my papers for school and built puzzles to pass the time. I had to leave her there to return to school and Jesse, but the NIH even flew her home because she was part of their study.

That was the year I found out that I got tenure, and felt that I had achieved something. I had set out and reached another goal, but like any other time in my life when I had done so, the feeling was empty. After the satisfaction wears off, the mind never needs long to find other problems. The mind tricks you into thinking, "This is your new, big problem, so think about this now, over and over again, or else you are being irresponsible." That is the main function of the mind, after all: to find out what is wrong and try to fix it. But that is also its main flaw, leading us to assume that something is wrong. Something is always wrong no matter what. Anyone who has ever achieved anything knows that the mind only needs a little while to discover, uh oh, another problem is creeping around the corner.

Chapter 9
Falling Back to Negative Stories

I went about my life, but I started to fall back into negative, mind-created stories. Even when everything was good, and no surgeries were scheduled in the immediate future, my mind gravitated toward doom.

I was smart, so I knew that it would be foolish to think that these surgeries were done. I would hear other people talk about their future and their extravagant plans for ten years from now and retirement, and I would get disturbed. I didn't want to think about the future ever, especially many years into the future. My mind told me I could never make any plans too far in advance. I never booked vacations more than a few weeks ahead of time, because who knew if a surgery would be needed, and we would lose our deposits if we couldn't go. Any time a thought crept in about Jesse's possible future needs, I would find myself in a panic, and I did anything I could to put it out of my mind. My mind pushed back.

Teaching school was a good distraction, but since getting tenure and getting comfortable in the classroom, even my job became second nature. To fill the void, my mind tried to solve the problems with my family, but those problems could only be solved when they came up. My mind didn't know that, so it would always say, "Think about those problems. You are not being responsible if you don't." I needed to find peace.

I had taken several courses and seminars that were designed to make me an enlightened thinker, but obviously, I wasn't enlightened enough. I started reading every book I could find on enlightenment. I read all the Deepak Choprah books. I read all the books from Carlos Castaneda, Dan Millman, and any other New Age author that I could find. I read books like *A Course in Miracles, Conversations with God,* and *The Four Agreements.* I read about the Dalai Lama and the Buddha. I am not a Christian, but I read many interpretations of the teachings of Jesus. I loved Eckhart Tolle's concepts on the mind and its stories. I even went to see Tolle live in the city one night. I listened to audiotapes from him and dozens of others constantly in my car. I was on a relentless search for truth and interpretations about what is so in this world.

I took seminars given by the Landmark Forum, and I took their weekend course called the Advanced Course, which was the continuation of the course I had taken many years earlier. During that course, I spent a weekend doing intense self-analysis, and faced all of my worst fears head on. I was able to see how everyone in the world is similar to me, and that I was not alone in my suffering. I met

Falling Back to Negative Stories

many others who had created the same kind of suffering but used different stories to get there.

I created a story about myself that I was an expert on the subject of enlightened thinking. I was able to achieve a kind of inner peace that I had never known before. The problems in my life were unavoidable, but the suffering I had endured was unnecessary. I gave myself permission to be happy again.

• • •

After I decided to give up my suffering, everything in life looked different to me. I loved working in a school where I could help so many kids. I vowed to help everyone around me wherever I was. I was committed to doing anything for anyone because helping others helped me. I had a great time with my classes, and I put on an elaborate show with jokes and music-infused lessons for them every day.

Jesse showed some talent for putting on a show himself, and we were so surprised when he sang a long solo in the play, *Bugsy Malone,* at the YMHA we belonged to. He also started running track at his high school. He was the slowest kid on the team, but Cathy and I cheered for him as he finished his three-mile races. I told him anyone could come in first in these things. Coming in last with pride showed more character than anyone else on the team. I told him it was the coolest thing in the world to come in last, and I meant it. Running the race is all that counts.

Cathy also loved teaching the kids in her school, and we had a year without any medical problems. We kept doing shows on the weekends, and I even got Jesse into the business. I bought speakers, mixers, microphones, and CD players, and started taking the DJ jobs that some of our customers requested. Jesse and I had a lot of fun trying to figure out how to be DJs. First, we just pretended we knew what we were doing, and after DJing a dozen parties, we decided that we were actually DJs. I wanted to create a business for Jesse that he could maybe do on his own when he was in college, and this was something cool. I started running myself, and I realized that if I didn't listen to my mind, I could push myself further than I ever imagined. During the 2009–2010 school year, I ran three marathons.

I created a possibility for myself that said I was strong, powerful, and confident, and no matter what occurred, I would handle it in the best way possible. I knew I was still living in the war zone, and the bullets would never stop flying, so I would at least make sure I would always have enough money to pay any expense. I committed to making enough money for Jesse, too, so that finances would never be a problem for him. I made up a story that I would leave him millions in case anything ever happened to me.

Falling Back to Negative Stories

* * *

Getting money was one of the only things I knew I could control in this world, and I loved the game of acquiring it. After all I had read, and all the suffering I had done, I gained a perspective on life that was uncommon among my acquaintances.

People often sought my advice, and I was usually able to help them by pointing out how their problems stemmed mostly from mind-created stories. I decided to slowly replace my remaining magician shows with an even bigger show.

I started writing a presentation to be an inspirational speaker. I thought I could do it for free a few times, and then start offering it in adult education catalogues. I did some research about the business and saw how some of these "motivational" or "inspirational" speakers were doing it. Some of them were getting five thousand dollars a speech, so I thought, this is for me. If I could do a few thousand of these shows, I would be set. I designed my presentation almost like my classroom lessons, including graphics, sound effects, and music, but this thing I made was not a typical lesson. It was my story. I was excited to give it a try, so I rented a banquet room at a Holiday Inn, set a date and time for the presentation, and started to spread the word.

I planned to fill the room, but my plans were interrupted.

Mind-created Stories Create Intense Suffering

In March 2010, doctors discovered another kidney tumor in Cathy that had to be removed. They were also concerned about a fast-growing tumor in her pancreas. They told us about a new study and drug that were helping patients by reducing the size of their kidney tumors. It could possibly reduce the size of a pancreatic tumor, as well. We wanted to try it, so the doctors started making plans to get her on the study.

A few weeks later, Cathy was on the phone with an NIH doctor discussing the results of her recent scans. I was in the bedroom when I heard her scream, "What!? What are you telling me?"

I got on the phone with the doctor, and he was explaining how Cathy's pancreas had to be removed. He explained that the tumor was growing beyond a critical size, and it had to come out. The tumor was located too close to the pancreatic duct, so the entire pancreas would have to come out. We had known that doctors were watching her pancreas tumor, but they never warned us that its size was about to put the entire organ in jeopardy. So, the news was shocking.

We understood what the experimental drug could do. We were hoping that Cathy would be able to start taking it. This had been our plan, and now we thought we would have to live with the knowledge that we could have saved her pancreas if only we had been on that drug a few months earlier.

We had gotten in the habit of setting ourselves up for the inevitable. If there was a way to keep surviving, we would rationalize how we were going to do it, and we would make it be OK. And yes, you can live without a pancreas. That was the first question we asked, and they told us that without a pancreas, Cathy would become a type 1 diabetic, and she would have to watch her blood sugar and take insulin. She would also have to take a pill every time she ate something to aid in digestion. It didn't sound great, but it wasn't a death sentence,

Falling Back to Negative Stories

and we would manage it, and she would live. We had to accept the possibility that Cathy would lose her pancreas, but we first had to make sure that we were doing everything we possibly could to save it.

To go on the study drug, we had to be aware that the drug takes three months to leave her system. They couldn't do any surgeries while she was on the drug because it could cause excessive bleeding. So if she was to be on it, and it didn't work, and then she came off of it, doctors would have to wait three months before any surgery could happen. This complicated the decision because they wanted to remove the kidney tumor before the pancreas because it was easier that way, and she would have time to heal for the pancreas surgery. We asked about the possibility of these tumors growing much larger during the six-month period that we would be trying the experimental drug. The doctors felt it was worth the try.

She went on the drug for three months, and her scans showed no change. The drug didn't work, at least not fast enough for our restricted situation. She had to wait another three months for it to leave her system, and then begin with the surgeries. We resigned ourselves, but then something happened that caused us to create a story that would cause us to question their diagnosis.

• • •

The doctors brought us into one of the little consultation rooms at the NIH clinic, and discussed Cathy's pancreas problem. A team of endocrinologists had already been discussing her case before the first doctor came in to consult with us. Through our many years of visiting the NIH, we have noticed that there are many levels of doctors. There are attending doctors that work on the hospital units. Usually they don't know the patients' full history. They only know what they see when they glance at the chart, and then move along to the next patient. There are resident doctors, and then there are surgeons. Usually the surgeons have several lower-level surgeons working under them. The chief surgeon calls the shots, and if a subordinate surgeon needs to consult with someone, they go to their chief.

The doctor who came in to see us this time had seen Cathy's scans and discussed them at length with his team, but he was not a chief surgeon. He was only a resident doctor studying under the chief of endocrinology. He explained that he had seen Cathy's scans, and predicted that she would be getting a Whipple operation. This is when the surgeon only removes a portion of the pancreas and leaves enough behind to perform the normal functions of the organ. This confused us, because until now, everyone we had seen during this visit to the NIH was telling us that she would be losing the entire pancreas. We told this doctor this, but he said he had looked at the scans and didn't see why the Whipple operation was not possible. Then he drew a chart showing exactly what it would look like after they rerouted Cathy's insides. He was very detailed in the explanation. He left the room, and Cathy and I were happy about what that guy had just told us.

Falling Back to Negative Stories

Then he came back with another doctor, his boss, the chief of endocrine surgery. The chief started the conversation very smugly, saying, "So we will be removing the entire pancreas." Cathy and I looked at each other as the higher-level doctor explained the procedure.

I listened patiently, and when he was done, I said, "So in your opinion, she definitely needs to have the entire pancreas out." He said yes. They had given us their opinions. We left the room, and Cathy and I discussed several things.

One doctor thought that a partial operation was needed, and the other thought differently. Of course the chief's opinion should be more valuable, but that didn't change the fact that a very qualified doctor thought a Whipple operation could and would be done. We had to get another opinion. This was too big of a decision to leave up to one doctor.

Besides, I didn't like the second guy. I didn't like his smugness. I recognized that I may have just disliked his information, and was making up a story to justify my agreement with the better prognosis. But what really happened is that one guy said one thing and the other guy said something else. There was no story involved in that.

We knew another doctor who used to see Cathy years ago at the NIH. He worked in New York now at Montefiore Hospital as the chief of endocrinology. We sent him the scans and made an appointment. Incidentally, Cathy's surgery was not an emergency. In all these years, we have never really experienced a real emergency. We always had time to think about what we were doing to manage Cathy's very complex condition—and for that, we were always grateful.

• • •

In June, Jesse said he was having a problem with his left hand. He was finishing his freshman year in high school, and he was on the track team. We noticed that while he was running, he wasn't lifting his left arm up as high as his right one. At first we thought he had twisted a muscle or maybe pinched a nerve—on a recent class trip, the kids were in the hotel pool, and he had a girl on his shoulders. When he came home he said he had hurt his neck, but the pain passed. But now his hand was hurting, and he was even experiencing some numbness.

I immediately knew what it could be, but I had to control my panic. It could be a symptom of VHL, or it could just be a pinched nerve. My mind wouldn't let the worst possible thought go, of course. His pediatrician didn't seem concerned, but sent us to an orthopedic doctor.

The orthopedic doctor wasn't sure what was causing the numbness. He sent us to another doctor who measured the nerve impulses from his neck down the spine and to the arms. We told both doctors about the girl on Jesses shoulders, and it seemed logical that he had pinched a nerve in his neck. The nerve doctor noticed irregular nerve activity in Jesse's arm. He sent his results back to the orthopedic doctor, and we went back and forth between these two doctors for the first few weeks of the summer. Nothing ever happens fast when these kind of things are being figured out by doctors.

We kept hoping that it was just a pinched nerve, but I had a sinking feeling for most of the summer. Jesse's hand was not improving and he was certain that it was numb. In August, the orthopedic doctor noticed that Jesse's left arm and the left side of his chest had less muscle tone then his right side. Jesse was always very thin, and we hadn't noticed it before, but when we looked at him with his shirt off, it was apparent.

I asked Jesse to leave the room. We had never discussed VHL. We never wanted him to create a story about himself that he had a problem. We wanted to shield him from it for as long as we could. I expressed my concerns to the doctor about the possibility of a tumor causing his problem. I explained what VHL is, because most doctors have not heard of it. This doctor thought that if a tumor were causing this problem, Jesse would feel pain near the tumor location; there was not, so the doctor didn't think it was a tumor. The doctor suggested an MRI of Jesse's head and spine to be on the safe side.

That gave me more hope, but I had seen a lot of doctors over the years. I knew the difference between the top ones and the ordinary ones. This guy was your everyday smalltime doctor, so I was apprehensive of his diagnosis. No one had said anything yet to make me panic, but I knew I was prone to panic, so I really had to keep taking this one step at a time. Constant worry would not help anything.

When the doctor saw the MRI results, he called Cathy. It was a tumor after all. He was sorry. He actually apologized to Cathy, and when I heard that, my mind started creating stories. When a doctor sees what you have, and says, "I'm sorry," it is very difficult to not create a negative story, especially when he says it about your fifteen-year-old son whom you love more than life itself. I had to fight off horrifying ideas.

The school year was starting, and I had to get myself together. Cathy, Jesse, and I all went back to our classrooms. Jesse had no fears yet because I didn't let him have any. He had confidence in his parents, and he knew he was in good hands. He knew Mommy always had operations, and he knew we never made them out to be a big deal, so if he did need one to fix his arm, he wasn't afraid.

I was afraid, though—very afraid. I would drive to work, my mind continuing its dirty work on me. Sometimes I yelled, "Shut the fuck up!" I tried as hard as I could to separate myself from my mind. There was too much I had to do, and I had to stay effective. I couldn't let my mind be in charge of the person I was. I would say out loud, "I'm driving this person, not you. I'm driving this vehicle (the vehicle being me), not you." I was turning into a crazy person, but I had to get out of the mind-created story.

• • •

We sent Jesse's MRI scans to the doctors at the NIH. They were the VHL experts, and if Jesse needed a surgery, I wanted him there. I managed to

Falling Back to Negative Stories

get through the first three weeks of the school year, and then I had scary phone conversation with the NIH.

I spoke to Hedde, the patient coordinator at the NIH who had discussed Jesse's scans with a team of neurology doctors. I knew Hedde because she had set up Cathy's appointments for years. Hedde told me we should get down there as soon as possible with Jesse. She told me to remain calm and take my time. I asked her why she was telling me that. I asked her about Jesse's tumor. She told me, "The tumors are big."

In all the years we had been going to the NIH, no one ever described tumors in such a way. The staff was trained not to alarm people, especially since patients were traveling long distances. "The tumors are big," she had said, and I tried not to dwell on it, but I called my principal and another teacher and told them what was happening. Our neighbor agreed to take our dog for as long as I needed, and I cried hysterically in her garage. She told me I had to be strong for them, and she was right. I was a wreck as I drove to Jesse's school to tell his principal. I knew I couldn't let Jesse see me like that, so I tried as hard as I could to pull myself together. After breaking down again in the principal's office, I composed myself, found Jesse, and on the way home I gave him the news that he would be missing school for a while, and we were going to the NIH to get his arm and hand fixed.

I called my mother to tell her what was happening, too. My mother, Sheila, is an enlightened person. She had done a lot of the work that it takes to get to a place of enlightenment, and still participates regularly in seminars and retreats that are designed to shine the light of awareness on our mind-created stories. Sheila and I have read many of the same books, and she has achieved peace and happiness in her own life. She knows that it took me a long time to get over the story I created about my past and my unusual teenage years. We have spoken about it many times, and any resentment I held toward my parents had been gone for many years. I needed my mother then. In my mind, I was like a small child who needed his Mommy to make everything be OK. I needed someone on this trip to the NIH to keep us out of the mind-created drama that would undoubtedly take us over.

Cathy, Jesse, Sheila, and I made the four-hour drive to Maryland, and got Jesse checked in as an NIH patient for the first time. Shortly after we got him settled into a hospital room, a doctor who had seen Jesse's scans came in to talk to us. He was a young doctor doing his residency under the chief of neurosurgery. He asked Jesse a bunch of questions, and then did a physical exam. The abnormality in Jesse's arm and hand was apparent, but when he checked the reflex responses on his feet, the doctor also said that there was irregularity there as well.

I was trying not to become frantic, and asked that doctor if he had seen where the tumors were. He said yes. Then I looked him in the eyes, and

Falling Back to Negative Stories

asked him if they could get them out. He said, "Yes, we can get them."

When the younger of two doctors told us about Cathy's pancreas tumors, the chief of endocrinology had told us something different. I repeated this story to Jesse's doctor, and asked him if his superior was going to tell us something else. He didn't answer me. He came back with the chief of neurosurgery a little while later, who seemed annoyed. He asked us if Jesse was aware of what was happening. When the doctors spoke alone to Jesse, I guess Jesse didn't seem afraid enough for them. We didn't want him to be afraid, and we had been through this sort of thing so many times with Cathy that we knew fear did not help anything. It seemed as if the doctor didn't think we had told Jesse about the seriousness of the situation. We weren't even completely aware of what was happening ourselves, but we told both doctors that Jesse knew there was a tumor that was affecting his arm and he would probably need surgery to get it out.

The chief of neurosurgery then told us something that still hurts, years later. He said he was reluctant to perform this kind of surgery without completely leveling with the patient. Now we were really scared, and asked what he would want to tell Jesse. He told us that the tumor in the brain was big, and the tumor on the spine was the biggest one they had ever seen. He told us that there was a strong possibility that Jesse could be completely paralyzed. He told us this in the coldest way I had ever seen a doctor speak to us, and he wanted to tell Jesse the same thing.

I would never let him speak those words to my son. It was Friday, and more scans would be done on Monday, and Jesse could stay with us for the weekend and check back into the hospital on Monday. After he gave us this news, the doctor told us to have a nice weekend.

"Have a nice weekend." How was that even possible? I was in a total panic.

I had to leave the building. I left Jesse, my mother and Cathy in the hospital, and I went across the street to the family lodge. I couldn't contain myself, and I did not want Jesse to see. How could I go a whole weekend, waiting to see what they were going to tell us on Monday?

A woman in the Family Lodge saw me crying. She explained to me that her daughter was here because she had some form of leukemia. She also shared how her son had died at twenty-five from the same thing. She told me I needed to be strong, but at the moment, I could not comprehend strength. She told me about another man she had seen years earlier who stayed in a panic all the time after receiving a poor prognosis for his son. She didn't think that man would survive the ordeal. She was religious with a strong faith. She said, "You can't control this. It's in God's hands. Just like my daughter's fate is in God's hands."

She was very calm as she spoke to me. She wanted to help me. I was never religious, but I did

Falling Back to Negative Stories

find myself asking God to help me many times during Cathy's surgeries. We always had positive outcomes, and even though I didn't believe any of what seem like myths professed by Christianity and Judaism, I could not help feeling like some sort of universal intelligence was out there. Maybe I just prayed when I was scared, but I did it on many occasions.

Praying wasn't helping me at that moment, though. I had to calm down. The woman told me, "If God decides to take my daughter, then he will take her. It has nothing to do with me." She was at peace with that, and I couldn't see myself finding the same kind of peace with the possibility. Yet my panic was hurting the situation. Her faith was helping her. She was empowered by it. All considered, meeting her helped me.

Jesse came back to the family lodge with us for the weekend. Cathy and I found it almost impossible to not fall apart in front of him. We would leave him with my mother and walk away into corners to cry. She would do the same thing when she wasn't around us. Jesse wanted to go to the movies, so we did, but I couldn't tell you anything about the movie we saw. I was so stuck in my head that I didn't even see it. We went to the zoo, and I walked around like a zombie. I couldn't eat a thing. My stomach was in knots, and I felt like I would throw up all weekend. Here I was, the guy who knew how to separate what was real from what was a story, and I was completely and absolutely absorbed by a mind-created drama. Of course, most people would say that everything

I was going through at that time was completely justified. I could get tons of agreement that I should be suffering. Only a cold-hearted person would say I didn't have to be in a state of shock and fear. But agreement wasn't helping me. And the suffering was killing me.

I couldn't sleep a wink. I couldn't forget the doctor's words. Cathy and I couldn't even talk about it. I don't know what she was feeling, but she was always tougher than me. She had faith in herself, but I knew that underneath her exterior calm, she was a wreck.

My mother had a friend of hers call me. The man led courses for the Landmark Forum. He was considered an expert in the transformation of human consciousness. I needed to get calm and effective, and having people tell me that everything was going to be OK was not going to work. The man's name was Angelo. My mother's husband had filled him in on our situation. Angelo had to first assess my level of enlightenment before he would know what to say to me. I understood that right away when he asked me which courses I had taken. I explained how I had taken three of the weekend courses offered by his organization. I told him about all the books I had read and the kinds of self-analysis I had done.

I guess he thought I could take some strong truths, so he let me have it. He told me that what was causing my panic right now had nothing to do with my son. He told me that what was causing my panic was based on something I had learned a long time

Falling Back to Negative Stories

ago. He told me that there was a time when I had something going on in my life that I didn't want to be happening. The feelings I was having now were a response to that, not to what was happening now.

I told him that my son could die. I told him that my son could be paralyzed. He told me, "If he dies, he dies, and if he's paralyzed, he's paralyzed. It has nothing to do with what's going on with you right now."

I realize that most people who are reading this now are probably thinking, "What an asshole. How could this guy possibly help someone?" But he was right. I couldn't control what was happening. I could only control how I was reacting. This realization brought me out of the story for a moment, and actually calmed me down. My mind told me I wasn't being a responsible father if I was not freaking out about this problem, but my mind was also keeping me in a state of panic, which was hurting the situation even more. The conversation with Angelo helped me.

• • •

Monday morning, Jesse had MRIs and scans of his entire body taken. Later we consulted with the doctors again. They saw that Jesse had smaller tumors on his kidneys and on the lower spine, but these were ones that would be watched probably for years. The big problem was the brain tumor and the spinal tumor. As we walked into the consultation room, the two neurosurgeons followed us. I turned around and told the smug one that I hoped he was ready to treat me for a heart attack, but he didn't seem to care about me at all. He was such a dick.

We sat around the table to discuss our options. The conversation started by addressing the fact that we hadn't told Jesse how serious the problem was, and that the doctor was reluctant to perform the surgery without full disclosure to his patient. We discussed nothing about how the surgery would be done or what exactly was involved. I was annoyed. I didn't know why our parenting decision was the most important part of the conversation. I asked if it was possible to get the tumors out, and Jesse would be OK. The chief of neurosurgery didn't answer me. There was a long silence. I asked again, and he said reluctantly, "Yes, it is possible."

My mind was screaming at me. My mind was recalling all the conversations I'd had with so many doctors over the years. I knew when I was talking to doctors who were confident in what they were going to do, and I knew when they weren't. This guy wasn't sure how to handle such a complex surgery. My mind was screaming, "He doesn't know how to do it! They don't want to tell you it could turn out OK because they really can't see a positive outcome here!"

That was the story I created. I couldn't renounce it as just a story, though. I had to make the right decision for my son, and I had to put him in the hands of the best possible surgeon. I was having a moment of clarity that was allowing me to take action, and in that moment, I left the conference room.

Chapter 10
How to Get What You Want

I left the building and ran alone across the street to the family lodge. I had a short period where I could stop thinking and start doing what I had to do. I started making phone calls. I called my brother and told him he needed to leave work immediately. He needed to pick up two separate sets of the MRI scans we had taken for Jesse in two different facilities in New Jersey. Once he had them, I would tell him where to bring them. I called the radiology centers to arrange to have those scans picked up by Keith. I called my brother-in-law, who was a doctor, and told him how the NIH guys could not see a prognosis other than paralysis. I told him to get on the phone immediately and find a top neurologist that was familiar with VHL. I called my friend Sue who was a nurse practitioner at Columbia University Hospital. I told her the story, and she started working for me, too.

Within an hour, I had two top doctors waiting to get Jesse's scans hand-delivered that day by Keith. Keith drove all over New Jersey and into New York City to help me. He would take off from his job as long as I needed him to. He was like my right arm, and I needed him to be by my side for this thing. I was going to get Jesse other options. I didn't care if I had to fly anywhere in the world or spend every dime I had. I had to create a better possibility than those doctors were giving me. I agreed to have one more consultation with NIH doctors, but I knew I would never let a man who didn't have my trust ever touch my son.

• • •

The next morning I could barely bring myself to get out of bed. I could hardly stand in the shower because my knees were shaking, and I threw up. I must have lost fifteen pounds in those three days, because I had scarcely eaten a thing. Looking at Jesse was excruciating. He didn't know what I knew. He couldn't know what I knew. I couldn't have him be in the same kind of panic I was in. He must have known I was a wreck, but I was still trying to hide it.

When we got to the hospital, the nurses said the doctors wouldn't be ready to speak to us for a half hour, so Cathy and I walked over to the hospital chapel. We sat in there and Cathy prayed. I know I pray different from her, but I asked God to please, please help my son. We did so for the entire half hour and then waited in the room the staff had reserved for Jesse. In the meantime, he waited across the street with my mother.

The two doctors we had been seeing were not coming. Instead, the director of neurosurgery came instead. His name was Dr. Lonzer, and he used to be the chief. Now he ran the hospital and gave speeches and lectures all over the country. Dr. Lonzer had performed both of Cathy's brain surgeries, and he entered the room with a calm demeanor. He told us we needed to lower our anxiety levels. He conceded the fact that Jesse's spinal tumor was the biggest one he had ever seen, and he was not sure whether the brain tumor or the one in the spine should be removed first or simultaneously. He said that many doctors have been debating how to proceed on this. He gave us the statistics based on past spinal surgeries. He said that seven percent of these types of surgeries lead to paralysis. He said that based on the size of Jesse's tumors and the location, his risks were higher. But he said that it could be done.

  He thought that the surgery should be done in New York. He knew we lived close to the city, and said that it was going to be a long ordeal, and that the ordeal would be better for everyone if it took place close to home. Then he said something that really calmed us down. He started talking about how after the ordeal was over, Jesse would still need to be checked frequently, and if he had facilities closer to home, he would be more likely to keep up with it. He started referring to when Jesse goes to college, and beyond. He referred to these future events as thought they would actually happen. He made the whole thing seem possible, and that was something we were not doing. We were so stuck in a negative story based on the other doctor's words that we saw no possibility for a future. I had prayed in the chapel for a way to come out of this nightmare, and after our conversation with Dr. Lonzer, the possibility was there. It really did seem like God had created a possibility for us.

Dr. Lonzer said they were not kicking us out of there, but if we wanted to check with other doctors, it wouldn't be such a bad idea—it just had to be done immediately. He gave us some names and some hospitals. One of the hospitals, Columbia, had just received Jesse's scans yesterday from Keith. It was hard for us to decide not to use the NIH after all its successes with Cathy, but we now knew we would leave there that day and find another hospital.

We felt a lot better, but during the drive home, my mind was working hard. My mind told me that the NIH didn't want to do it because the chief of neurosurgery probably thought I would kill him if the operation failed. I may have given him that impression. My mind told me that maybe the NIH wasn't the top place to go anymore. My mind made up a story that since their funding had been cut in the last few years, maybe they couldn't afford to take a case like ours, which could possibly cost over a million dollars. My mind kept analyzing all the conversations we had with the NIH doctors, and the one doctor's horrible words rang over and over in my head.

Jesse was confused about why we were leaving, because we always told him how great the NIH was. I told him there were better doctors in New York, and it was better that we be closer to home. He didn't believe me, and he was getting mad.

• • •

How to Get What You Want

I kept e-mailing my school during those weeks. The school year had just started, and I was in no condition to come in to work, not until this thing was over. I sent e-mails to my principal and my teacher friends explaining the situation, and one time I even sent one that said, "I fear the worst is happening, and I can't talk about it." My friends at the school were going to handle anything work-related for me. I was also taking an online grad school course at the time. I was in the middle of getting my master's degree in teaching. I had to call the college and tell them my papers were going to be late.

It was better to be home after that week at the NIH. It was calmer, our dog was there, and we could sleep in our own beds. I was still in a panic, though. My thoughts about that one doctor kept popping in my head. If he believed these tumors could not be removed without terrible consequences, then he may have been right. He was the chief of neurosurgery at the NIH, even if he was a dick. I would wake up in a sweat in the middle of night thinking about it.

A neurologist recommended by my brother-in-law received and went over Jesse's scans with her team. She called me and offered the possibility of using several different drugs in combination with radiation therapy. She did not believe his spinal tumor could be removed surgically; she considered it inoperable. It was very hard to not attach myself to the mind-created story that came with this diagnosis, but I had to let people say what they would and then know that the words were spoken, and meant nothing more.

The story that Jesse's tumors were inoperable kept presenting itself in my head, though.

My friend Sue, the nurse practitioner at Columbia, referred us to Dr. Feldstein. I went to his office with Cathy, my brother, and my brother-in-law, Joe. I wanted Keith and Joe there to hear everything that was said so that we could compare our stories about the conversation later.

We gathered in Dr. Feldstein's office. Sue sat in, and another doctor listened in, as well. Dr. Feldstein was familiar with VHL, but he wanted Cathy and me to give a detailed explanation of Cathy's medical history. As we laid out the complicated history of kidney surgeries, brain and spinal surgeries, and all the complex eye procedures, we realized how much Cathy and I had been through over the years. Sue later told us how amazing it was to hear how matter-of-factly we were able to discuss what had happened to us. The room was moved by our medical story, but everyone knew that Jesse's present condition was bigger than anything we had ever dealt with.

Dr. Feldstein appeared to be a brilliant man. He had been grappling with Jesse's scans for a day or two, and he told us his plans for attacking the tumors. As he explained the procedure he wanted to do, he seemed to be thinking out loud—he used terms and references that he knew we didn't know, but saying it out loud was clarifying his ideas in his head. He was very scientific about it, and he referenced many other cases. His plan had four steps to it. There was a procedure called embolization. The doctors send a probe in through the arteries, and the probe somehow reaches the tumor and leaves a glue-like substance that freezes up the tumors so they can't bleed during surgery. Bleeding during this kind of surgery was a big deal because if they took out the brain tumor first and fluid came down into the spinal tumor, it could cause huge complications.

So, the plan was to freeze the brain tumor, and then take it out, and then freeze the spinal tumor, and then take that one out. The surgeries wouldn't be done at the same time. Apparently that was too risky. The embolizations would be done the day before each tumor would be taken out, so the whole process could theoretically be done over the course of a week or two, first the brain then the spine.

Dr. Feldstein told us that the whole thing was fraught with all kinds of risks, but he also showed us how the spinal tumor was wrapped around the spinal cord, and this would really be his only chance. He spoke with deliberation and confidence. It seemed as if he was more concerned with his own thoughts on how this would be done than being able to express them in terms we could understand, but I could tell that this guy was an expert, and we knew we wanted him to do the surgeries.

Cathy, Keith, Joe, Sue, and I were in complete agreement. The doctors at the NIH never even talked about embolization. We found out later that Dr. Lonzer at the NIH, Dr. McCormick, recognized as one of the top neurosurgeons in the country at Columbia, and Dr. Feldstein had been conferencing about this matter with some of the best neurosurgeons in the world. We literally had the best people in the world working to save Jesse from paralysis—or worse.

Dr. Feldstein needed to make sure all the doctors were on hand when the surgeries took place. Since the process of doing all four procedures would be done over a week, Feldstein wanted everyone available, especially for the final procedure when the spinal tumor would be removed. They scheduled the first procedure to take place in two weeks. From then on, Jesse would stay checked into the hospital until it was all done.

This gave us two weeks at home. I would not go back to school. I couldn't leave him. I didn't know if this would be the last two weeks I would ever spend with him. I felt confident that we were putting him in the best hands. I felt like these procedures could go well. I had seen Cathy endure so many of them, and everything always worked out.

I wanted to hang on to that optimism, but my mind would tell me otherwise. My mind would remind me of the NIH doctor's pessimism and uncertainty. I would tell myself to also remember how Dr. Lonzer spoke about Jesse going to college and living his life. My mind would remind me that Dr. Feldstein couldn't make any guarantees, and there were no odds on this procedure working. My mind constantly reminded me about what could go wrong, and I would scream at it to shut up, but it wouldn't. My mind was my worst enemy.

• • •

I had to focus on the present moment during those two weeks before the surgeries. I said to myself, "Nothing bad will happen today. Today, everything is still OK." I spent every moment with Jesse. We went out to lunch every day, and I bought him anything he wanted, mostly X-Box games and videos. I prayed constantly. I had never done this before, but I was not taking anything for granted. I was desperate, and I understood why people become religious. I wanted everyone I knew to pray. I wanted to put as much positive energy into Jesse's situation as possible. I sent an e-mail to the staff at my school asking them all for their prayers.

I found myself worrying about how I would survive through these surgeries. I thought a lot about how I would bear it while it was happening. I didn't want to have a heart attack while he was in surgery, and I worried about that, too. I had to just walk through this, survive for Jesse, and be there no matter what happened. I had to take it one thing at a time.

The concept of Zen is based on doing one thing at a time because you can never really do more than that in each given moment. Usually the present moment is very simple. It is when you start to contemplate all the things you need to do in the future that the present moment becomes complicated and troublesome. I needed to just focus on what I was doing and only what I was doing, and I would be able to live through those two weeks with as little thinking as possible.

• • •

We arrived at the hospital for the first procedure: embolization of the brain tumor. The doctors needed to freeze that tumor up so it would not bleed when they took it out. We behaved confidently around Jesse. We were qualified to prepare him, telling him stories about Cathy's successful surgeries—how they always seemed so scary beforehand, but a few weeks after they were over, it was like they never happened.

We watched them wheel him away, knowing that this would be the easiest procedure of the four. It had to work, though, because the rest of the complicated plan depended on it. We sat nervously for a few hours in the waiting room. Cathy got into a discussion with a cancer patient, and they regaled each other with war stories. We always talked to the other patients in waiting rooms, and we could probably write a book about the tales we have heard.

Dr. Feldstein came out to report the news: So far, so good. He was able to embolize the brain tumor, preparing it to be safely removed. Step one complete.

The next day was the brain surgery. I felt OK because I had helped Cathy through two brain surgeries. My mind told me to be worried about fluid flowing down into the spinal tumor and causing damage, but really, what would worrying do? I told my mind to go fuck itself.

The family came to the hospital to wait out the procedure. Everybody talked in the waiting room about regular things—politics, work, and everyday concerns. I struggled to talk to anyone, just wanting this thing to be over and move on to the next step. I prayed and sent an e-mail to my work friends to do the same. My mother had a cardinal at the Vatican do some praying, too.

And in a little while, Jesse came out with a big bandage around his head. The surgery went well. The brain tumor was gone. They also started to do some work around the spine to prepare for the bigger surgery. They needed to cut through all the muscles in his neck to make it easier to reach the spinal tumor. This would take time off the long spinal surgery a few days from now. Dr. Feldstein said his neck would swell up like a balloon and it would be very painful for a while—and man, was he right.

When Jesse got his breathing tube out and was back in the critical care unit, he was trying to get comfortable. He kept saying, "I can't get comfortable. I can't get comfortable." In fact, he was in excruciating pain. I am in pain just writing about it now. It was the most painful moment of my entire life so far, standing next to him and not being able to do a thing to help him. He had to endure it. I had to remind myself, *All that matters is that he survives.* Whatever pain he had to tolerate didn't matter.

He was so weak after the brain surgery. He couldn't move his left arm at all, and now his right one was numb, too, but the second step in the process was over. Cathy and I never left the hospital. We were both sleeping on chairs in his room, and I hadn't slept for more than a few minutes for days. Jesse needed constant care from the nurses, and the machines he was hooked up to never stopped beeping.

The next step was to embolize the spinal tumor. Jesse had to be put to sleep again for the third procedure. We waited. We could barely talk to each other. Again, like every other part of the process, this had to work. It was like we were living in the Holocaust, and we were completely exhausted not knowing what to expect from day to day. I met a woman in the waiting room who had a son whom they realized had late-term leukemia all throughout his body. Her son was Jesse's age, and his prognosis did not sound good. She was a Hassidic Jew, wearing the customary clothes, and she was surrounded with others in the same garb. I explained to her how I was not a good Jew because I married a Catholic girl. She told me I was a good Jew. She said she would pray for Jesse, and I promised to pray for her boy, Raphael Abraham. I kept my word, and I know she did, too.

Dr. Feldstein came to see us after the embolization was done. He said they were able to embolize most of the tumor. They monitored the nervous system up and down the spine during the process to make sure the embolization was not causing changes in his system (or this is how I understood it, anyway), and when they started the process on certain parts very close to the spinal cord, it had caused problems, so they stopped. The way Dr. Feldstein described it, the surgery was starting to short out Jesse's electrical system. He was worried that when they reached that part of the tumor during the surgery, such a short-out might happen.

He gave us a very technical description of how the surgery would be done, and during his description, he pointed out many possible problems that could occur. It was a horrifying analysis of what could happen, but he was sure that if they did not do it now, the tumor would be virtually impossible to remove. It was so hard not to be terrified after what we just heard, but we went right back into Jesse's hospital room, and said, "OK, three quarters of the process is over, one more part to go."

Jesse was not happy at all. He never smiled, and he didn't care about watching TV or doing anything. Those days in between surgeries were long and painful. I sat on the chair next to his bed and read the e-mails of support from my friends. One night I noticed my nephew had a famous friend on his Facebook page. The guys name was Mike Sorrentino, and he starred on an MTV show called *Jersey Shore*. He was known as The Situation. The Situation's status said he was going to be in New York City that week.

I'm not sure why I did it, but I sent him a private message explaining my son's situation, and I asked him to stop by Jesse's hospital room since he would be in the city anyway. Jesse was a fan of the TV show, so I thought it might cheer him up.

Believe it or not, the guy's agent called me the next day, and The Situation came to visit Jesse the night before the big surgery. Jesse was amazed that the guy standing in his hospital room was the real Mike Sorrentino. It was the first time Jesse smiled in a week. He even had us put his cell phone on so he could tell all his friends.

Mike, The Situation, did a really nice thing for us. All the nurses were going crazy when he came, and after that, every time someone would come in to our room, they would say, "I heard The Situation was here." Dr. Feldstein had never heard of him, but the younger doctors on his team explained who he was.

The morning of the spinal surgery Jesse seemed so weak and fragile after what he had already been through, that it seemed impossible he could even survive such a procedure, going into it in such a battered condition. It was the scariest thing that had ever happened to any of us—me, Cathy, my parents, my brother and sisters, and Cathy's family. Everyone was there to wait it out with us. Cathy and I could not speak. We sat in Jesse's hospital room, white as ghosts, for eight hours. Cathy repeated the St. Jude Novena over and over again. She lay there with her head in my lap as our family kept walking past, leaving us alone.

How to Get What You Want

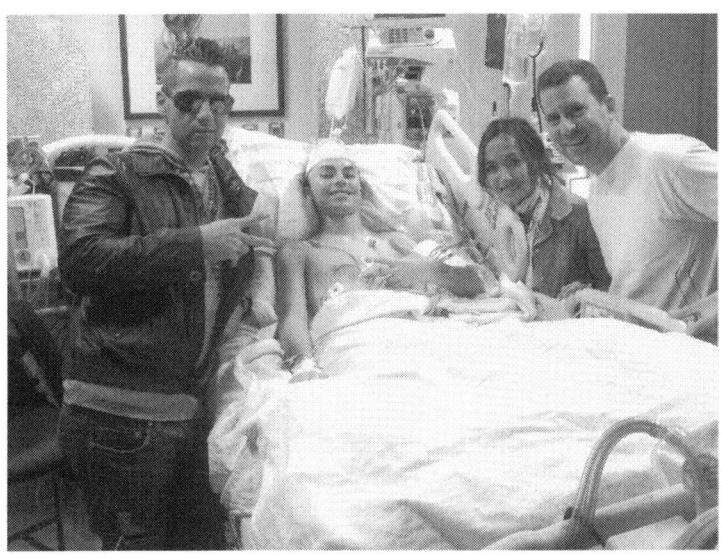

• • •

For weeks, I had feared living through these hours. My mind kept throwing thoughts into my head of Dr. Feldstein telling me horrible things after it was over. I prayed. Our friends prayed. Jesse's high school prayed. My and Cathy's schools prayed. My whole family prayed as they never had before.

I walked downstairs and stood in front of the hospital for a while with my brother. Columbia University Hospital is located on the outskirts of a poor neighborhood by Harlem. There were so many homeless people asking for money with cans in their hands. They all seemed so angry. They were walking around with their story of how life had dealt them a bad hand, and they had no idea how lucky they were. They could walk and breathe and eat, and they had no idea what a gold mine they were sitting on with their good health. Everyone was suffering with what they thought was a big problem in their lives.

Keith and I were coming up the elevator when Cathy called my cell phone. Ernie, Cathy's father, saw one of the nurses and had news to share. I exchanged a look with Keith in the elevator, knowing the news was coming. He hugged my shoulder.

The nurse told Ernie that it went well. I know that nurses don't say that unless it was true. It wasn't going to be the horrible news my mind was trying to force on me. I held Cathy and we exploded in sobs and tears. Everyone that stood in that room was crying, and I can't even describe the feeling of relief that came over me. I had to get the full news from Dr. Feldstein, so I ran over to the surgical waiting area to get any information I could. I saw an anesthesiologist who was in the room during the surgery. She was smiling and she said that it went very well. My mind immediately created a story that said that the whole room must have been high-fiving each other—they must have been so happy about completing one of the most complicated spinal surgeries in history with such perfection. I knew it was just a story, but there was no way that someone could walk out from a surgery, grinning as the anesthesiologist was, and not be proud of their work.

Dr. Feldstein emerged a little while later, and our family greeted him like a hero. He explained how smoothly it went. He said he knew that he got the whole thing, and Jesse's neurological condition was considered athletic, meaning there was neurological function throughout his body. Feldstein was a small, bald, Jewish man, but to us he was a god, explaining how he performed his latest miracle.

Every single member of my family hugged him. My sister-in-law said, "I like you more than the Situation any day."

• • •

This is an e-mail I sent to the staff at my school after the surgery:

Hello everyone,
As you know, my son had brain surgery last week and a spinal surgery yesterday. The tumor on the spine was the largest one they had ever seen. Most doctors would have considered this tumor to be inoperable, and even some doctors I sent his MRI films to told me that. The prognosis we were receiving was horrible, and we have been living in a nightmare for over a month now. We were fortunate enough to find an amazing man, Dr. Neil Feldstein, who was able to assemble a team and devise a very complicated plan to remove this tumor. Even Dr. Feldstein knew that the procedure had many possibilities for many big problems to occur, but there were no choices in the matter—it had to be removed. The description of this high-risk surgery was horrifying to hear. Those of you who know me well know that I am not

a religious man, but I have been praying so hard this month, and I know so many of you have been praying for my family. I am so happy to be able to tell you today that yesterday a miracle occurred in that operating room. They were able to remove the entire tumor without one single complication. None of the anticipated problems came up, and it went as smoothly and perfectly as it possibly could. Even the doctors were amazed. Jesse is still on a breathing tube, but his neurological functions are intact. Dr. Feldstein is very optimistic for a full recovery. We need him to regain his ability to swallow and he will need some rehabilitation for moving his arms and legs, but he is already getting noticeably stronger.

Thank you all so much for your love and support during this time. It has meant the world to me.

Hope to see everyone very soon.
—Greg

Chapter 11
Jesse's Recovery

We rejoiced in the surgery's success, but we knew Jesse had to recover. We were not out of the woods yet, and the recovery was not what we expected. I questioned if I had sent out my celebratory e-mails prematurely.

Despite how well the surgery went, a tumor that big on his upper spine wreaked havoc on Jesse's little body. These are some of the things I had to watch my son go through after the surgeries were over: I had to watch him be trapped with a breathing tube for seven days. I had to watch him struggle to break free of this incredibly uncomfortable predicament. I watched him bite through his breathing tube twice only to have the doctors force it back in. I had to watch his lung collapse after the breathing tube finally came out, and I had to watch in the middle of the night while they did a procedure to repair his lung. I had to watch as they put a trach in my son's throat, knowing that it might never come out. I had to watch him lose almost fifty pounds, until his arms and legs were like twigs and his full body weighed seventy-nine pounds. I had to watch his arms flail around as he tried to make them work again. I had to watch my beautiful boy's spirit almost completely disappear. I had to listen to him beg me for a drink and something to eat, and I had to watch him struggle with a swallow that wouldn't work. I had to know that he might never swallow again—we had to suction out his saliva every five minutes, so he wouldn't drool all over himself. I had to know that he might never eat or drink again. I had to know that he might never be able to walk or use his arms again. I had to accept these things as they were happening, but I had to hold on to the possibility that everything could come back and he could be whole again.

My friend, the Hassidic woman, was still watching the doctors perform all kinds of procedures on her son. We were going through the same kind of pain, watching our sons suffer without knowing what the final outcome would be. She always had lots of family around. They prayed in an organized way with prayer books and people chanting things in the waiting areas. They all knew who I was, and they would walk up to me and tell me they were praying for Jesse.

One night, all the chanters gathered in her son's hospital room, inside the ICU. It was obvious that the boy was dying. I went out into the waiting area, and saw my new friend crying. I looked her in the eyes, and I will never forget the expression on her face. I could not even attempt to console her. There were no words. I could not help feeling strangely guilty because we were both praying so hard for our boys, and her son was gone, but mine

Jesse's Recovery

was not. My son would live. The next morning she and her whole family had disappeared from the ICU as if they had never been there.

• • •

The attending doctor on the unit told me that Jesse had no indication of swallowing whatsoever. She said he didn't even have a gag reflex. I asked if it was permanent, and she said maybe. She was actually telling me that my son might never eat or drink again, and he might have to be fed through a tube for the rest of his life.

I went outside and cried. I was trying so hard to look at the reality of the situation. What was real was her words, and that I was making a terrible prediction based on what she said. That was really happening—nothing more. I held on to the possibility that he would swallow again, and the next day, Dr. Feldstein told us that he thought the swallowing would come back.

It was an emergency for weeks in the critical care unit. The doctors could never tell us what would improve. They don't do that. They never want to give false hope, so whatever his current condition was, Cathy and I had to accept it as possibly permanent. I couldn't do it, though. I had to accept that I couldn't accept Jesse's current condition, and would do whatever was possible to get him better.

I was qualified to help my son. When I was in college I had taken a course in fitness training with my brother and father. My brother became a wellness coordinator for Prudential, and he currently gives seminars on fitness throughout the country. My father was a competitive bodybuilder—he placed second in the 1963 Mr. Universe contest, and has been working out for his entire life. He is probably the fittest seventy-year-old man most people have ever seen. Since the course we took together, I had done nothing with my fitness trainer certificate, but I was impressed by the potential of the human body and how it could be trained.

    I have always worked out regularly at the gym. Just a year prior, I had run three marathons. When I started my running regimen, I could barely run half a mile. I built up to a full mile, and before I knew it, I was running five miles every day. I built up to ten miles, then fifteen, then twenty, then three marathons. I knew well how the human body could be enhanced through the power of intention. I worked Jesse's frail body as much as he could tolerate. I had him push and pull his muscles every day. As long as there was the slightest bit of strength in any one area, I knew the possibility for more strength existed.

"Is Anything Possible?"

    Our friends reached out to us like crazy. We received hundreds of messages and e-mails. My friends from work visited the hospital and forced me to take an envelope with thousands of dollars in it. My old partner, Dave, whom I had barely seen in twenty-five years, sent Jesse a brand new iPad. I actually wrote a lot of this book on it. Lots of other friends sent Jesse all kinds of gift cards and electronic devices to keep him busy, but so far, Jesse was unable to use his hands to do anything.

People offered me anything and everything. We had good insurance because Cathy and I were both teachers, but if I needed to, I could have raised a million dollars. I know now what it feels like to be George Bailey at the end of *A Wonderful Life*, because that is how everyone we had ever known came out to support us.

During the toughest of times when Jesse was fighting to breathe or just fighting the claustrophobia from being trapped under a breathing tube, Cathy and I would hold up signs reminding him to fight. We had signs all over the room that said, "Fight the urge to freak out." "Don't stop fighting." We had a big poster set up above the TV that quoted Sylvester Stallone from *Rocky*. It said, "Nothing hits harder than life, and it will knock you down if you let it. It's not how hard you can hit, it's how hard you can get hit and keep moving forward."

When Jesse would do his feeble workout, which really was him just pressing his arms and legs against my hands, I would play the *Rocky* theme in his room. Jesse loved Rocky, and I needed him to be Rocky. He was in the fight of his life. Jesse asked me to get Rocky to come to his room. I guess he figured if I could get the Situation, I could get anyone.

I sent a Facebook message to my old roommate in college, Julian Levi. Julian was a visual effects producer in Hollywood, and he did a lot of work on some big films. I knew he knew movie stars. Julian called me as soon as he got my message. I hadn't spoken to him once in almost thirty years, but he worked hard trying to get Sylvester Stallone to show up in Jesse's hospital room. He couldn't pull it off, but the fact that he would do that for me showed me how good friends never leave you. My only job in this world was to inspire my son in any way possible, and if that meant making crazy requests to people I hadn't spoken to in years, I would do it.

• • •

Jesse's mind was not helping him. His mind was telling him to be mad and freak out, especially when doctors and nurses were inserting painful things into his body. He was fighting it and actually hurting himself. He bit through his breathing tube twice, and those things are almost indestructible. The doctors caused him more pain because they had to put the tube back in. When he came back to the room after having the trach put in his neck, he was flailing around and freaking out. The doctors needed him to calm down. His heart was racing and his blood pressure was way too high. His pulse was almost at 200.

Jesse understands what I mean when I distinguish between the mind and the self. There was a whole team surrounding Jesse, and I put myself next to his ear. I told him, "Your mind is telling you to freak out right now because you are in pain. Your mind is saying to fight, but you are hurting yourself more by fighting. You don't have to freak out. You

Jesse's Recovery

are not your mind. You are in control of this situation right now. Now I want you to lower your heart rate. Lower it, lower it… Lower your heart rate." The doctors and nurses stood silently, amazed as Jesse's heart rate went down from 200 to 160 to 120 and eventually down to 90, all in the span of just two minutes. One of the nurses later asked me, "What was that?" I told her, "I'm not sure what that was, but it worked." Jesse had calmed himself down by taking control of his body.

After being in the hospital for a whole month, Jesse's breathing, blood pressure, and heart rate normalized, his collapsed lung stabilized, and his incision was healing. He was in a bed all the time, though, so his body was a stick, and he could barely move. Dr. Feldstein decided that Jesse should not be moved to a regular hospital room because he needed to start rehabilitation immediately. The trach was still in his throat. There was still a feeding tube in his nose. He still couldn't swallow and required suction every five minutes. He couldn't even sit up without being in excruciating pain. His hands and arms were useless, and we had no idea if he would ever be able to walk again.

He was discharged, and Cathy and Jesse took an ambulance over to the Children's Rehabilitation Hospital in New Brunswick, New Jersey. I followed in my car. I had checked it out a few days earlier, and they were well equipped for extensive rehabilitation. And any change of location was good.

Almost every child in this new facility was in a wheelchair. Some of them were severely disabled. When Jesse was wheeled in, it looked like he was the weakest, frailest child in the whole place. He was still connected to a lot of things. He had a trach and a tube running from his neck for oxygen. He had respiratory meter attached to his finger, a feeding tube running out of his nose, and sticky electrodes attached around his chest to measure his heart rate. It was very uncomfortable for him still. The surroundings had changed, but his physical predicament remained the same.

They started him on physical therapy right away. The first thing he needed was to be able to sit up. He could only do it for a few minutes at a time. It was painful and he would get dizzy immediately. They fitted him into a wheelchair with very specific design just for him. Those first days in rehab were all about getting him to tolerate being in the wheelchair and sitting up. We started with just five minutes at a time. I had to carry him out of the bed and put him in the chair. He was as light as a feather. We worked our way up to fifteen minutes and then a half hour.

I wheeled him around and around the hallways of his floor. We had to take the electric suction machine with us always so that I could suck out his saliva as it built up. We did laps around the floor every day, and he always asked to stop by the full-length mirror so he could see what he had become.

• • •

Jesse's Recovery

Cathy still had her own problems. We told the NIH what was happening with Jesse, but we couldn't wait too long to have the tumor on her kidney removed, because we still had to address the pancreas problem, too. The first week Jesse was at the rehab hospital, I stayed with him, and Cathy drove to Maryland with her sister for a kidney surgery at the NIH hospital.

Our whole family was living in hospitals with us. My mind told me that Cathy's surgery was overwhelming all by itself, but I didn't need to listen to that bullshit. She would be fine. This was her fourth kidney surgery, and she was a pro at it by now. Cathy checked in to the hospital, had her surgery, recovered and a week later, she was back in New Jersey. She stayed with her sister for a few days until she felt well enough to join us in our adventure.

I slept on the little couch next to Jesse's bed every night. I was never going back to work until he got well. I would never leave him. I would walk away from my tenured teaching job. I would sell my house if I had to. I would spend every nickel I had ever earned if I had to. These things became absolutely real possibilities.

We continued our laps around the floor. Jesse wondered if his neck would ever stop hurting. His legs seemed strong, and whenever I would lift them or bend them, he could apply fairly strong pressure in every direction. Swallowing became the biggest issue. Unless he could swallow, he could never eat or drink. Unless he could swallow, he could never gain the muscle weight he needed to get stronger. They fed him Ensure and water through his feeding tube, and that was all the nutrition he received. The other kids on the floor got meal trays three times a day, and Jesse longed to eat with them.

He received swallowing therapy every day. They would attach electrodes to his neck and do something called VitalStim therapy. The electricity was supposed to stimulate the muscles around his throat and the therapist was giving him all kinds of strategies to re-learn how to swallow again.

Jesse had barely any strength in either of his hands, and he couldn't control his arms. He had a tray on his wheelchair, and as I wheeled him around, I had him try to use the iPad so he could check his Facebook messages. He was getting tons of messages from his friends at school. So many kids were telling him how much they loved him and wishing him well. My whole family was looking at the messages he was getting, and they couldn't believe how many great friends he had. Jesse didn't want any of his friends to see him, though, not in his present condition. He fumbled around with the touch-screen keyboard and at first he could barely spell out a single word, but he improved quickly. The touch screen on the iPad actually proved to be great occupational therapy, because he didn't have the strength to push down a key on a regular keyboard.

The therapists at the rehab hospital were excellent. He got occupational therapy for his arms and physical therapy for his legs. They worked together to strengthen his core. It was key for him to just be able to withstand sitting up before they could even try to have him stand. Strengthening the core was also essential for strengthening the muscles around his neck and throat for swallowing. I would watch his skinny little body on the mats in the gym struggling to move up and down. I watched him always. I wanted to make sure I always knew what he could do so I could help when the therapist weren't there, which was most of the time. Even if he received therapy for four hours in a day, which was a lot, we were still there in the hospital all day, every day.

Just us being there was essential. I walked him around for hours every day, having him use his fingers and helping him strengthen his core. We pushed and pulled against his arms and legs in his bed. I made him squeeze my hand constantly. The extra therapy he got from me and Cathy was just as essential as the therapy he got from the professionals. He was improving in all areas. He was getting stronger.

One day a radio station came to the hospital. They were interviewing the staff and patients on the air to raise money for the hospital. Jesse was interviewed on the radio, and he explained everything that happened to him. They took a picture of him in his wheelchair with a feeding tube in his nose. He was amazing on the radio. He was always very confident about his recovery, because he had no stories about why he wouldn't recover. After he was done being interviewed, we wheeled him to the back of the room, but Jesse wanted to show off his new trick. Jesse stood up from his wheelchair and slowly and carefully walked to the table where the radio hosts were sitting. I cry every time I remember that moment.

Jesse's appearance on "WCBS 101.1 FM—New York—Bob Shannon and Joe Causi Making Miracles Happen"

• • •

Swallowing became the biggest issue in all of our lives. We had to get Jesse to swallow. Everything about his recovery depended on it. My mind always remembered the doctor who told me she didn't know if the swallowing would ever come back, but I shut that thought out every time it entered my head.

Jesse's Recovery

In fact, swallowing was more important than walking. Without it, he would forever drool and never eat or drink. If I could have, I would have given away everything I ever had just to get Jesse to swallow.

His swallow therapist, Kate, had a real heart for Jesse, too. She saw how he was beginning to move the necessary muscles, but it was never enough to actually get something down, not even his own saliva. She brought in another specialist who knew how to perform something called deep pharyngeal neuromuscular stimulation (DPNS), a process that stimulates the pharyngeal musculature. Melissa was certified in this technique, and she and Kate worked together every day putting the electrical stimulation on Jesse's neck and sticking cotton swabs dipped in lemon down his throat. It looked like they were trying to choke him, but they were seeing a better swallow beginning to happen.

Jesse's breathing was normalizing, as well. They capped his trach, and he didn't need oxygen anymore. One day the doctor came in to our room, looked at Jesse's chart, and said, "It looks like you don't need this anymore." He pulled the trach right out of Jesse's throat as if he were casually plucking out his golf tee after a teeing off at the golf course. He put a Band-Aid on Jesse throat, said, "That will heal up soon," and then he walked out of the room. We all were so happy to see that thing go. We hoped that without such an obstruction in his throat, Jesse's swallowing would dramatically improve.

• • •

I would wheel Jesse down to the meditation room every day. I have seen healing processes done during seminars and retreats. I have seen instructors perform these processes and make people's headaches or backaches instantly disappear. I believed that the body had an intelligence of its own, and it was capable of healing itself.

In the quiet atmosphere, I would tell Jesse to imagine an energy ball in his throat. I would describe the energy ball like a green marble that was emanating light and healing energy. I would have him picture it in his mind and imagine it very intently in different locations of his throat. I would have him move the energy ball up and down his throat. I would speak very calmly and try to convey to him that I knew exactly what I was doing, and that each part of the process was designed to work. I needed him to really believe it would work. I needed him to use the powers of his brain that had never been utilized before. I needed him to tap into his own healing ability to help his arms and his throat regain their function.

As the trach hole in his throat healed, Jesse's swallow was getting better. Finally at one of his sessions, Kate and Melissa were able to see and hear an obvious swallow. He swallowed his own saliva. They worked hard to continue the progress, and I kept doing the visualization in the meditation room. Jesse needed less suction now, so he must have been swallowing more of his own saliva, and the girls started giving him ice chips to try. He struggled to

Jesse's Recovery

get them down, but he loved trying. Jesse had not eaten or drunk anything in two months, and I will never know the pleasure it must have been for him to just have a tiny taste of cold, fresh water.

After a few more days, Jesse was able to consciously start swallowing his saliva, and all of a sudden, he didn't need suction any more. He lived for the ice chips during swallowing therapy, and soon, he was able to swallow them all. They wouldn't permit him food or water, though. He could aspirate if something went down the wrong pipe, which is what caused his lung collapse in the critical care unit. The only way to be cleared for eating and drinking was to pass a special test where they can see, through an x-ray, all the liquid and food going down his throat.

Jesse worked hard to be able to pass the test. He worked with the girls, and we took our own private visualization therapy very seriously. He was becoming a proficient swallower again, and Kate felt confident that he would at least be cleared to eat strained foods and water.

We wheeled Jesse over to the Robert Wood Johnson Hospital, which was connected to the rehab hospital. This was one test we didn't want to fail. I could see the insides of Jesse's throat on the x-ray, and everything the doctors gave him to eat and drink went directly into the right place. The doctors cleared Jesse to eat anything.

Jesse had been dreaming about drinking a Mountain Dew because he kept seeing it in commercials, so on the way back to his floor, we stopped at a vending machine and got one. Kate supervised him at lunch that afternoon, and Jesse ate a whole turkey sandwich and a piece of cake. Kate said that she really didn't expect him to be able to eat like this so quickly, but he could do it, and she never saw someone's swallow come back so strong from the place it had been before. She said it was really like a miracle.

Cathy, Jesse, and I were in the business of making miracles happen. I sent an e-mail to my friends at work, "Jesse can swallow." My friend Kerry later told me that the message found its way through the entire school in about five minutes, making every teacher in the building's day. Who would have guessed that Jesse swallowing would be the biggest deal in the world?

I went out every day to buy him anything he wanted to eat. We were making a lot of friends with the other patients, too, because I kept bringing back burgers and pizza and chicken wings and anything else Jesse wanted. I was so happy to have a food party for everyone every day. Jesse was eating everything in sight, and I was eating more, too—until now, Cathy and I felt guilty about eating, and we never let him know when we were having a meal.

Jesse gained weight fast—really fast. I had the nurses check the scales because it appeared that Jesse had gained twenty pounds in one week. Sounds crazy, but it was true. And the next week, he gained another ten.

• • •

Jesse's Recovery

We had spent Halloween, Thanksgiving, Christmas, and New Year's in the hospital. The way things were progressing, I was able to start thinking about my life outside of this situation. I hadn't worked in three months, and I was afraid if my absence continued much longer, I could lose my job. I needed the insurance. As for grad school, I was actually keeping up with the work. I sat next to Jesse's bed, working on my laptop, and actually completed two entire graduate courses while we were there. It gave me something to do other than worry, and I earned my master's degree three months after we left the hospital.

The trach was gone. The feeding tube was gone. Jesse was getting better at walking, and soon the wheelchair would be gone. We had a discharge date for January 3, and we used those final weeks to bring Jesse as far back to his old self as we could.

I sent out another e-mail to the staff of 100 teachers at my school:

> Hello everyone,
>
> I just received the three holiday baskets Kerry left for us. Cathy, Jesse, and I are overwhelmed by your generosity and thoughtful messages. I cannot express how much it has meant to receive your support and love for all these months. Your e-mails, cards, (Nancy dropping off cakes at our house), phone calls, prayers and well-wishes have kept us going with the knowledge that

there were so many people completely committed to us and our well-being. Jesse is progressing much faster now. He is walking and swallowing. After not eating or drinking for two months, he has miraculously progressed to being able to eat a regular diet. He is eating everything in sight, and I have been taking incredible satisfaction in watching him enjoy the simple pleasure of eating pizza, french fries, cakes, and everything else he wants and has been dreaming about for months. He has gained thirty pounds in just a few weeks, and with the weight, he is getting stronger. We are scheduled to be discharged from the hospital on January 3, and he will be getting outpatient therapy after that. I am arranging several other therapists to come to the house daily in order to bring him all the way back to his former self. I plan on returning to school on January 10. I wish you all the best for the holidays and new year, and I am looking forward to seeing everyone and getting back to my normal routine. Again, thank you, thank you, thank you, for all you have done.
 —Greg, Cathy and Jesse

Chapter 12
Scars

We came home and started to put our lives back together. Cathy and I went back to work. My father took Jesse to an outpatient physical therapy center in the mornings, and then kept him at his art gallery during the day.

My father, Jerry Winick, had about five tumultuous years after his divorce. Those years were my teenage years. By now, Jerry had pulled his life back together. He has been remarried for thirty years now, and he owns and operates Pencilworks Studios in Little Falls, New Jersey, where he teaches art classes, draws, and sells his own pencil drawings. My father, Jerry Winick, former second-place Mr. Universe, is also renowned as one the best pencil artists in the world, now giving me two big stories to brag about being his son.

This is one of my dad's many drawings.

• • •

Jesse was not ready to return to school for a few months after coming home. His days were busy with physical therapy, hanging out at my dad's gallery, and then getting tutored at home in the afternoons.

I took him to the high school track where he and I used to work out. We started out real slow, and it didn't take long before his walking and balance got so perfect that he could run. We started running one quarter-mile lap around the track and then two and then more. By the summer, Jesse and I were running three miles a day every day. Now, Jesse runs without even the slightest limp, and we are planning to start training for a marathon together soon.

As for me, it was difficult to return to work after our long ordeal. I felt lucky that I was able to come back to work with a story that had a happy ending. I never forgot my friend who lost her son or the many kids who were still dealing with unfixable problems at the rehab facility. I work in a very large school, and everyone was coming up to me giving me a big hug. I felt so loved by so many people. Even so, people just didn't know what to say to me. They were so scared of the possibility that such things might happen in their own lives that nobody even wanted to think about my experience, let alone talk about it. People live as if illness is not real, as if death is just a bogeyman who will haunt but not touch them.

One of the other things I noticed about being back in the real world was how seriously everybody took unserious things. The teachers were worried about the latest negotiations and budget cuts. Those are real concerns, but they hardly seemed worth so much stress. It's only money, but people were yelling and getting all bent out of shape about it in the teacher's room. I saw teachers who were just as mad and upset about budget cuts as I had been about Jesse's condition during our most intense periods in the hospital. I would still wake up in a sweat in the middle of the night remembering how horrible it was when Jesse couldn't get comfortable and I could do nothing to take away his pain. The teachers weren't as fortunate as me to have perspective lurking in their heads all the time. Without it, everyday concerns do seem like huge problems. Until the day when you wake up to reality and realize that none of those things ever really matter, you walk unconsciously through your life, thinking that every little development is monumental.

• • •

Throughout our ordeal, my mind never stopped supplying me with negative thoughts. That was my constant condition. It is everyone's constant condition. Something is always wrong. There is never a moment when the mind cannot find a problem to focus on. I had to continuously defy this condition in order to get what I wanted.

I am not saying that you can always get what you want. I met too many people in that hospital who were not as lucky as we were. We must accept what cannot be changed and make the best of it. What other choice is there, other than complaining about how things are and being miserable? I don't know what is possible in this life, and I cannot say that anything is impossible. I do know that creating a new possibility is easy. Just say it and do it, and if it doesn't work, say something else and do that. As long as you are alive, you can figure out a way to do almost anything.

The definition of a warrior is one who is engaged in or experienced in battle. Cathy, Jesse, and I do worry about the future. We cannot help it.

Scars

We know we will always have problems to deal with. We don't claim to be strong or confident. We do, however, know from experience that we are resilient. We know that we are warriors. We will face the future, and whatever comes, and we will fight, and we will make the best of reality.

The summer after we left the Children's Rehabilitation Hospital, Cathy had her pancreas removed. She is now a diabetic, and she is getting used to it. It is not a problem. Jesse and I walked into her hospital room after her surgery with t-shirts that said, "No Pancreas. No Problem."

• • •

I have said several times that I feel like I am living in a war zone. That is an interpretation my mind created. It is a story. Many people might agree that the metaphor fits and makes sense, but their agreement doesn't change the fact that it is a mind-created interpretation. Its purpose is to produce drama. It produces drama in this book I have written and it produces drama in my life. It makes what has happened harder to deal with.

You could argue that virtually everything I have written is merely a story, and there is very little truth or reality in it at all. The *real* story of my life could be explained in a few sentences: "I had to work to support myself when I was young. I opened up several businesses. I went back to college as an older person and became a teacher. I had to endure watching my wife and son live through many surgeries, and I wrote this book." That is all that really

verything else that I wrote was an inter-
those events, a dramatic, mind-created

I have to be very careful not to get absorbed in my complex story. All those things that have happened to me are just that: things that have happened to me. They are not me. They are events and situations. I am not my story. I am not a recollection of events. I am not my mind. I am much more than that. I am the awareness behind my thoughts and memories. I am the driving force that decides what I will do next. I am the creator of new possibilities. The possibilities that I create do not have to be based on the negative or positive stories that I have about myself. I can create possibilities that are not based on what I think I can or cannot do. All I have to do is create it, and say it, and it can be.

Suffering

The stories we create never, ever go away. I used to think that I wasn't enlightened enough because I could not stop the stories from coming into my head. My father would tell me how proud he was that my youngest sister Michelle was building up such a large bank account. She had been saving since she was young, and now as a young adult, she had saved almost a hundred thousand dollars. I cannot stop the story I created when my father drained my bank account as a kid, and I cannot stop my mind from thinking how I could have saved so much, too, if he hadn't taken all my money. I cannot stop from thinking how much easier my youngest sister had things. Every time my mother talks about the things she bought and the places she goes, I can't stop my mind from replaying its stories about how easy she has had things, being married to a millionaire for thirty years. Her life may not really be so easy, but I can't stop those thoughts from popping up. Every time I hear someone reminiscing about playing sports in high school, I hear my sob story about never having that experience because I was working all the time.

These stories pop into my head even if the situation has nothing to do with the past. The faintest similarity will bring them out. They are still so prominent in my head that even when I was dealing with our struggles with Jesse in the hospital, those childhood stories still intruded on my thoughts. I couldn't help thinking that if I had been in Jesse's situation when I was a kid, I surely would have been dead. I don't know why that thought would come into my head, but it did. I'll never stop being that little kid from so many years ago because my mind is not designed to delete things. Once I decide something for myself, that's it; it's there, and it never leaves.

Even the new stories that I built as an adult are here to stay. Every time a supervisor questions me about my teaching methods, I immediately recall my first supervisor and what a hard time she gave me. I can't help my inclination to get defensive. Every time we meet a new doctor for Jesse or Cathy,

I recall the doctor who gave Jesse his horrible prognosis. Anything that reminds me of that experience can send me back into a panic as if it were happening again, right now.

The fact is, our negative stories never heal. We will carry those scars forever. That's why some older people can be so cranky—the more stories they have created, the more scarred they become. The amazing thing is that everyone writes these stories all day, every day. Our natural inclination is to either create a new story about something or to live in a story created in the past. The only way out of it is to realize that you are doing it, and then the story loses all its power over you, because it is not real, and you can see it as only a thought.

I have known what is to suffer. There have been many times in my life in which I have endured almost unbearable periods of sadness and fear.

When I have observed the source of my suffering in those moments, I noticed that much of that suffering flowed from exaggerated, mind-created stories.

I can get lots of agreement that my suffering was justified, and often that agreement has been satisfying and made me feel loved by those trying to console me. But the agreement with and justification for my suffering has also served to fuel a story that I *should* be suffering.

The things that have happened were very real, and I am not saying that I could have reacted otherwise. Nor am I saying that a person is capable of renouncing emotion. Everyone must endure the hardships and sometimes the horror that this world can produce. The things that actually happen are hard enough, but often we tend to embellish difficult and tragic situations with our mind-created stories.

I have learned that I am not a positive person. Saying so would be a lie. My power to lead a positive life lies in the ability to see the negative thoughts and identify them as just that—thoughts. If I got absorbed in those thoughts, I would not be able to create positive possibilities. I could just believe the negative thoughts, and take them for reality, and then live into that reality.

The true power to create positive possibilities comes from outside the mind. It comes from the self, the person you are behind your thoughts. In every moment, you have the choice to live into the reality of negative or positive thoughts, or live into the possibility of something else entirely.

In 2011 and 2012, after all the big surgeries were over, Cathy, Jesse and I had a "normal" school year. We had a great time being teachers and affecting the lives of our students. Jesse had roles in four of his high school plays, and we got to enjoy watching him attend many parties and the junior prom. We never forget for a minute how fortunate we are to live such extraordinary lives

Made in the USA
Middletown, DE
24 November 2019